THE NORTH FIGHTS
THE CIVIL WAR:
THE HOME FRONT

J. Matthew Gallman

The American Ways Series

IVAN R. DEE   *Chicago*

THE NORTH FIGHTS THE CIVIL WAR: THE HOME
FRONT. Copyright © 1994 by J. Matthew Gallman. All rights
reserved, including the right to reproduce this book or portions
thereof in any form. For information, address: Ivan R. Dee, Inc.,
1332 North Halsted Street, Chicago 60622. Manufactured in the
United States of America and printed on acid-free paper.

Library of Congress Cataloging-in-Publication Data:
Gallman, J. Matthew (James Matthew)
     The North fights the Civil War : the home front /
J. Matthew Gallman.
          p.   cm. — (The American ways series)
     Includes bibliographical references and index.
     ISBN 1-56663-049-5 (alk. paper). — ISBN 1-56663-050-9
(pbk. : alk. paper)
     1. United States—History—Civil War, 1861–1865.   2. United
States—History—Civil War, 1861–1865— Social aspects.
3. United States—History—Civil War, 1861–1865—
Economic aspects.   I. Title.   II. Series.
E468.G35 1994
973.7'8—dc20   93-47471

The North Fights
the Civil War:
The Home Front

To my students,
past, present, and future

Contents

Preface   ix

PART ONE. TO ARMS!

1   Mobilization   5
    The election of 1860. Secession and calls for compromise. Fort
    Sumter. To arms! Political preparation. First Bull Run.

2   Two Nations at War   22
    Population and economy. Society and culture. Military
    organization and war aims.

PART TWO. HOW A FREE PEOPLE CONDUCT A LONG WAR

3   Military and Political Adjustments   39
    Success in the West, stalemate in Virginia. 1863: high tide
    of the Confederacy? National politics and the challenges of
    war. The 37th Congress. Politics at mid-war.

4   Manpower Adjustments   56
    Military organization. The state militia draft. The shift to
    federal conscription. Who served?

5   Emotional and Intellectual Adjustments   74
    Loss. Separation. Society and culture.

6   Economic Adjustments   92
    Supplying the military. Funding the war. Economic ebbs and
    flows. Individual economic experiences.

7   Patriotic Adjustments   109
    Interpreting voluntarism. Organized benevolence. Civil War
    medicine. Propaganda and ritual. Changes and continuities.

8   Racial Adjustments   125
    Emancipation. Black troops. Southern freedpeople. Free blacks
    in the North.

9 Politics in the Streets   141
   Political dissent. Violence. Politics in the Confederacy. Women in public.

PART THREE. THE ROAD TO VICTORY

10 Total War in the North?   159
   A modern military machine. The election of 1864. An increasingly powerful state? A voluntaristic machine? Free blacks in a changing America.

11 Victory and Its Legacy   178
   Three Sundays in April. War and the federal government. Economic growth and development. Community experiences. Gender roles. Race and class relations. Continuity and change.

A Note on Sources   199
Index   205

Preface

THE AMERICAN Civil War occupies a special place in the national memory. The popular fascination flows from many sources. More than 620,000 citizen-soldiers lost their lives in the war, dwarfing the human cost of any other American conflict. When the war finally ended after four long years, fundamental questions about the nation's future—and its past—had been answered. Still, Americans' deep absorption with "the people's conflict" is largely owing to its epic qualities. The heroes—Lincoln, Grant, Lee, Jackson —enthrall us. We pace monument-covered battlefields in search of distant sensations. Images of the dead gaze back at us from this, our first photographed war. The rhythms of the marching songs remain familiar to this day.

While the world away from the battlefield appears on the periphery of most Civil War narratives, this book places the Northern home front at center stage. The focus forces a rethinking of the war's immediate and long-term significance. In the process, our understanding of some of the principal players will change. But in a larger sense the war's main lines and its epic quality persist.

To understand the Civil War home front we must consider both how individual Northerners experienced the war years and how the North collectively reacted to the conflict's challenges in its communities, organizations, and businesses. This book brings together the war's national, local, and personal stories in a single narrative.

The months between Abraham Lincoln's election in late 1860 and the First Battle of Bull Run the following July saw Northerners move rapidly through a series of emotions:

from calls for compromise to cries for vengeance; from lighthearted optimism to grim resolve. In those first months Americans began to mobilize for civil war. After First Bull Run, Northerners settled into the more complicated business of adjusting to a continuing conflict.

In the first days of July 1863 three important episodes changed the direction of the war: the Union Army halted Robert E. Lee's second invasion of the North at Gettysburg; Ulysses S. Grant finally succeeded in capturing Vicksburg, Mississippi, the key to controlling the Mississippi River; and New York City erupted in several days of violent rioting triggered by the federal draft. During the war's final year and a half the Union—under the direction of Generals Grant and Sherman—perfected the strategies that later historians have called "total war."

Each chapter in this book embraces a particular set of historical questions, but a few larger themes recur. First is the matter of the Civil War as a catalyst for change. Certainly such a cataclysmic event left its mark on the North. But how great was this mark? What aspects of life changed, and where can we find evidence of continuities? For instance, how much did the Civil War accelerate the tendency for government—both local and national—to play an increasing role in everyday life?

A second set of questions concerns the war years as an evolving experience. How different was July 1861 from May 1863? From March 1865? Were there patterns of change that cut across different sectors of home-front life? And how were these related to the military experience?

Participation in war efforts is often credited with enhancing the postwar positions of previously powerless social groups. A third theme underlying many chapters is the wartime experience of Northern women, blacks, and immigrants. How did the positions of these groups evolve during the war years? Were they able to parlay wartime participation into long-term change?

One final interpretive theme runs through much of this analysis. Although I concentrate on the Northern home front, the discussion invites frequent comparisons with the South. Such comparisons are useful in that they suggest both the significance of the North's superior economic capacity and the critical importance of the regions' different cultural traditions.

This book is the product of more than a decade of work on the Civil War home front. The Note on Sources at the end of the volume only touches on the list of scholars from whom I have learned over that time. I thank my colleagues at Loyola College in Maryland for creating such a congenial atmosphere for working and learning. A Loyola College Faculty Development Grant enabled me to complete the manuscript. I am indebted to Charles Cheape, Stanley Engerman, Robert Gallman, Phyllis Gorfain, Reid Mitchell, and Thomas Pegram for their comments on style and content. I also thank John Braeman and Ivan Dee for inviting me to join the American Ways series and for their editorial suggestions.

J. M. G.

Baltimore
January 1994

The North Fights
the Civil War:
The Home Front

PART ONE

To Arms!
From the Election of 1860 to First Bull Run

THE MONTHS FROM late 1860 to July 1861 saw the United States change from a single nation, often at war with itself, to two nations bracing for a long conflict. Three critical episodes marked this transition. In November 1860 Republican Abraham Lincoln won the hotly contested presidential election, prompting secession by the states of the lower South by the time of his inauguration. The following April, after months of Southern conventions and Northern maneuvering, soldiers of the seceded Confederate states fired on the United States flag at Fort Sumter, South Carolina. In many Northern eyes this transformed the people of the infant Confederacy from wayward brothers into audacious enemies. Suddenly calls for compromise gave way to angry demands for vengeance. Three months later, as the Union's ninety-day volunteers neared the end of their enlistments, two untested armies clashed outside Washington, D.C., near Manassas, Virginia, and the small stream called Bull Run. When news of that chaotic battle reached the home front, Americans on both sides began to settle into the grim realities of warfare.

1

Mobilization

WHEN AMERICANS WENT to the polls in 1860 they faced a new, quite dangerous set of alternatives. Sectional conflict had been with the nation since its infancy, but never before had it so fully rent the fabric of American politics. Many Northerners rallied to the upstart Republican party as a fitting response to decades of indignities at the hands of the Southern slave power. The Republicans had emerged in the mid-1850s as a Northern coalition bringing together ex-Whigs, disenchanted Northern Democrats, antislavery Free Soilers, and nativist Know Nothings. In 1856 the party nominated famed explorer John C. Frémont, who ran on a platform emphasizing opposition to slavery in the territories. The Republicans carried an astonishing eleven of sixteen free states, but Pennsylvania Democrat James Buchanan won easily by taking the entire slave South—with the exception of Maryland, which went to the new American party's Millard Fillmore—and by sweeping the lower North. When Republicans met in Chicago in 1860 they nominated Abraham Lincoln, a man with a strong following in his native Illinois but with only a modest national reputation. They also sought to improve on their 1856 showing by offering a more moderate platform, including a firm denunciation of John Brown's recent raid on Harpers Ferry, and by catering to the industrial lower North with proposed tariff reforms.

While the Republicans, with their safe hold on New

England, sought to court more moderate Northerners, the Democrats suffered the fate of a national party with distinct regional wings. When they met in Charleston that April, many Democratic delegates called for the nomination of Illinois Senator Stephen A. Douglas, but the party's Southern wing refused to accept Douglas and called for a strong statement defending slavery in the territories. After the majority rejected the Southerners' slave code plank in favor of the pro-Douglas platform, the Southern delegates walked out of the convention, dividing the only national political party and one of the few remaining institutions that crossed regional lines. In June the Democrats reconvened in Baltimore, but they were unable to resolve their regional differences. The Southern "fire-eaters" walked out again and staged their own convention, nominating Kentucky's John C. Breckenridge. The loyal Democrats nominated Douglas. As the national political system threatened to come apart at the seams, a group of ex-Whigs and ex–Know Nothings joined together to form the Constitutional Union party, dedicated to preserving the Union. They nominated John Bell of Tennessee, who ran on a platform that essentially ignored the vital slave issue.

The election of 1860, as four years earlier, shaped up as two regional contests. But this time no candidate could claim a national following. In the North and West, Lincoln battled Douglas in a rematch of their 1858 senatorial campaign. In the South, Bell took on Breckenridge. When the votes were tallied, Lincoln had swept the North and West with 54 percent of the vote—including more than 60 percent in much of the upper North—and all but three of the 183 free-state electoral votes. But Lincoln received less than 40 percent of the popular vote and did not even appear on the ballot in most Southern states. Breckenridge won most of the slave states, receiving a total of seventy-two electoral votes, while the Constitutional Union candidate Bell took thirty-nine electoral votes in the upper South. Douglas finished second in the popular election with nearly a million votes (35 percent), mostly from the free states, but managed only nine electoral votes.

As Abraham Lincoln prepared to take office, Americans wondered about the man they had just elected. Those who met the president-elect consistently remarked on his great height and his unusually homely, angular appearance. Born in a Kentucky log cabin, Lincoln taught himself law while developing a strong passion for politics. At twenty-five he was elected as a Whig to the Illinois state legislature, where he served two terms. Later, as a young congressman, he attacked the Southern Democrats who pushed the nation toward war with Mexico. Stephen Douglas's Kansas-Nebraska Act helped lead Lincoln into the new Republican party; the Supreme Court's 1857 *Dred Scott* decision, protecting slavery in all the territories, left him further convinced of the threat posed by the Southern slave power. In 1858 he gained a broader national reputation in a series of open-air debates with Douglas during their senatorial campaign.

Lincoln scholars have long debated his political beliefs and his thoughts on slavery in particular. We know he was distressed by the "peculiar institution" from an early age. But whereas radical abolitionists demanded immediate emancipation, Lincoln—clinging to a hope that the slave system would die on its own—joined the more conservative voices who called for colonizing Africa with freed slaves and compensating slave-holders for their lost property. In his debates with Douglas he adopted a moderate stance, to the left of his opponent, calling for an eventual end to slavery and for some aspects of racial equality, but insisting on white dominance. As a candidate for the presidency, Lincoln vowed to resist the extension of slavery into the territories. And although advocating no immediate challenge to the institution where it existed, Lincoln did insist that the nation could not forever exist half slave and half free.

To many Southern observers the election's message was clear. The North had chosen a representative of a party explicitly opposed to Southern interests, a candidate who did not even appear on their ballots. Most knew nothing of Lincoln the man, but they immediately recognized his election as a threat. Talk of secession soon dominated public discourse. Some Southerners urged the slave states to pursue a joint response while radicals in the Deep South demanded immediate, unilateral action. At a secession convention in December, South Carolina's 169 delegates voted unanimously to leave the Union. Within two months most of the lower South had followed suit, all voting for secession by large majorities. In February 1861 representatives from the seceded states met and formed the Confederate States of America. Jefferson Davis, the new Confederate president, immediately authorized the formation of a 100,000-man army. Thus only three months after Lincoln's election and while Democrat James Buchanan still occupied the White House, the Deep South had already left the Union and was poised to fight for its independence.

As Southerners debated their next move, President Buchanan proved himself an ineffectual leader in crisis. In December 1860, in his final annual message, the Pennsylvania Democrat straddled the fence, announcing that secession was illegal while insisting that he had no power to "coerce" the rebels back into the Union. In Buchanan's eyes the villains were the radicals on both sides: the abolitionists and the fire-eating leaders of the slave power.

With the Deep South leaving the fold, Northerners debated various measures to appease their adversaries. Buchanan's own plan called for a constitutional amendment protecting slavery, an end to the Northern states' personal liberty laws that protected fugitive slaves, and even the acquisition of Cuba, an island long on the South's list of objectives. Kentuckian John Crittenden—who would soon have sons serving as major generals on both sides of the conflict—proposed a set of constitutional amendments that would turn the clock back a decade or so. The Crittenden Compromise called for an extension of the Missouri Compromise's 36°30' line all the way to the Pacific, with slavery to be preserved south of it; the permanent protection of slavery in Washington, D.C.; the guaranteed preservation of the interstate slave trade; and enforcement of the Fugitive Slave Law. Both compromise schemes sought to convince the South that the Republicans' victory did not signal a new wave of encroachments on slavery. The hope was that such assurances would appeal to Southern unionists, leading them to break ranks with the secessionists.

These calls for compromise had broad appeal in the North where the commitment to the Union was often much deeper than any antipathy to slavery. Still, the Republican leadership was loathe to sign away the fruits of electoral victory. Lincoln, meanwhile, adopted a fairly moderate stance. The president-elect was unwilling to give up his commitment to restrict the expansion of slavery into the territories, but he was ready to promise to enforce existing legislation. The first task, Lincoln felt, was to keep the eight upper South slave states from seceding long enough for the South's antisecessionist forces to coalesce. In mid-February the fate of those border states remained unclear as representatives from both the federal and Confederate governments pleaded their cases. The secessionist momentum slowed when Virginia, Missouri, and Arkansas, at state conventions, rejected the secessionist appeals while Maryland's unionist governor refused even to call for a convention. But for Lincoln such victories were tenuous.

As Inauguration Day approached, the Northern citizenry grew increasingly restive at the prospect of permanent disunion and the likelihood of armed conflict. Although the Republican leadership managed to ward off the congressional compromise proposals, calls for peace—whatever the cost—rang out in many communities. In February state representatives from the North and upper South met in Washington for a "peace convention" and endorsed measures close to Crittenden's plan. In many cities business leaders who depended on trade with the South demanded conciliation without coercion. These voices were joined by an unusual set of initiatives by Northern workers. In the aftermath of the disastrous Panic of 1857, organized labor had fallen into disarray; but by 1860 several national unions had reemerged, and in some places workers had begun to meet in citywide assemblies. In December 1860 workers staged a mass meeting in Louisville, Kentucky, to declare their support for compromise and the preservation of the Union. The following month Philadelphia's unions sent delegates to a citywide meeting of workingmen that passed similar resolutions. On Washington's birthday, labor delegations from the upper South and lower North congregated in the City of Brotherly Love where they called for conciliation.

The sweep of national events proved too great for these calls for compromise. But during the critical weeks between the formation of the Confederacy and Lincoln's inauguration, many in the North united in their call to preserve the Union, even if that meant catering to Southern demands. Although soon to be set aside, the spirit of conciliation sparked spontaneous demonstrations throughout the North and succeeded in bringing together organized workers even where their economic goals had failed to yield such cohesion.

Before his inauguration Lincoln embarked on a whistle-stop tour of the Union's major cities; his arrival in Philadelphia coinciding with the workingmen's assembly. While the laborers called for conciliation, Lincoln raised a new flag at Independence Hall—commemorating the admission of Kansas into the Union—and drew applause by promising that "the Government will not use force unless force is used against it." On April 4, 1861, the president-elect took a

carriage to his open-air inauguration where he was introduced by Oregon's Senator E. D. Baker. As he delivered his
Inaugural Address, the Capitol loomed behind him, its
dome still under construction. Lincoln promised an enthusiastic audience that he would not interfere with slavery in the
South but would "hold, occupy, and possess" federal proper-
ties in Confederate territory. One observer praised the "conciliatory—peaceable—but firm" tone of the speech, adding,
"Let the Southern hotspurs say what they will, it will have
more tendency to bring back the seceding States than
anything else that could have been said." That October
Major General E. D. Baker would die at the Battle of Balls
Bluff.

As he took office Lincoln resolved to walk a tightrope. By
protecting federal property he would maintain the Southern
symbols of Union as a beacon to loyal Southerners. But in so
doing he had to avoid giving the appearance that the young
Confederacy was under attack. Unfortunately for Lincoln,
off the coast of South Carolina events were moving very
quickly. While Northerners were debating compromise plans,
Major Robert Anderson and a garrison of eighty soldiers
manned the still unfinished Fort Sumter on an island in
Charleston Harbor. In January President Buchanan had
tried to reinforce the fort, but the ship *Star of the West* was
forced to turn back when the South Carolina militia opened
fire. By the time Lincoln took office the fort's supplies were
dwindling, and the issue was coming to a head. Some
insiders advised Lincoln to evacuate the fort to buy more
time, but Radical Republicans insisted that this would imply
a recognition of the Confederacy. They called on the president to use force to protect this vital symbol of the federal
government.

On March 30 Lincoln directed the military to prepare
plans to reinforce both Fort Sumter and Florida's Fort
Pickens. When the relief mission finally departed for the
South on April 4 it carried supplies but no armed men.

Consequently, when Lincoln informed South Carolina's governor that the rescue boat was underway, he was able to characterize it as a mission of humanity rather than an act of aggression. The burden of action thus fell to South Carolina. If it let the relief ship in, Fort Sumter could survive indefinitely. If the rebels used force to resist, they would be firing on an unarmed vessel.

The Confederates viewed the fort through their own symbolic prism. To them it represented a "foreign" military power looming off their shore. To capture both the federal forts would affirm the Confederacy's autonomy. Moreover, any armed conflict was likely to lead the recalcitrant upper South into secession. As the relief ship approached and an anxious nation looked on, the Confederacy ordered Major Anderson to surrender Fort Sumter. When Anderson refused the demand, Confederate guns opened fire at 4:30 a.m. on April 12. After thirty-four hours of shelling, Anderson surrendered the fort without losing a man.

The fall of Fort Sumter sent shock waves through American society. On April 15 Lincoln called for 75,000 volunteers to serve for ninety days. Two days later Virginia seceded rather than fight against its Southern brethren. Arkansas, North Carolina, and Tennessee soon followed. In the North, Lincoln ordered the blockade of Southern ports and took measures to keep the remaining border states in the Union.

What had happened? The nation had stumbled into an armed conflict that would last four years and cost more than 620,000 lives. Yet only a minority of Northerners welcomed serious warfare, particularly over the issue of slavery. In the months before the firing on Fort Sumter, many citizens favored conciliatory measures toward the rebels while others were perfectly happy to let their Southern neighbors go unmolested. Certainly the majority of Northerners who cast votes for Lincoln in 1860 never reckoned on the consequences.

As soon as the firing began, these voices of caution gave

way to rabid patriotism on both sides. But once again the
enthusiasts badly underestimated the stakes. In his call for
volunteers for only three months, Lincoln revealed a central
assumption of policymakers North and South: if there was
to be war, it would not last long. In response to his
constituents' fears, one South Carolina senator promised to
drink any blood shed by the conflict; the *Charleston Mercury's*
editor vowed to eat any bodies that fell during the war.
Once it became evident that lives would indeed be lost, the
Confederates counted on their superior military skills and
their stronger national will to carry the day. Meanwhile,
Northerners calculated their tremendous numerical superiority and concluded that the upstart Confederacy would
soon collapse. But for this advantage to persist, the Union
would have to control the remaining border states.

With Virginia gone to the Confederacy, Northern attention turned to Maryland, Kentucky, and Missouri. The loss
of Maryland would leave the Union's capital isolated and the
North's transportation system badly disrupted. This vital
state represented a microcosm of much of the nation's
diversity. To the south and along the eastern shore, plantation owners leaned toward the Confederacy; the more urbanized Baltimore area was home to moderate unionists.
When other Southern states held secessionist votes, Maryland's unionist Governor Thomas H. Hicks had refused to
call a convention.

On April 19, 1861, the 6th Massachusetts Volunteers
entered Baltimore, bound for the defense of Washington.
No rail lines passed through Baltimore, so the troops had to
march across the city to board the southbound cars. As the
green troops passed, a secessionist mob set upon them. A few
soldiers fired into the crowd. The ensuing riot left four
soldiers and a dozen locals dead. In the aftermath of the
Baltimore riot, local citizens—led by the pro-Southern police
chief—tried to block future troop movements by tearing up
railroad tracks, burning bridges, and destroying telegraph

lines. Northerners voiced astonishment at the outrages in Baltimore. On the night of May 14 the Union Army occupied Federal Hill overlooking Baltimore. Marylanders who voiced secessionist sentiments risked arrest as Lincoln used his war powers to suspend the writ of habeas corpus, allowing for arrests without charges. In Annapolis Governor Hicks called a special legislative session which voted against secession. This vote reflected both the emerging unionism in the state and the presence of a strong military force outside the statehouse.

The successful control of Maryland was vital in political and logistical terms, though an estimated twenty thousand of the state's fifty thousand soldiers ended up fighting for the Confederacy. Lincoln waged similar battles for control over Missouri and Kentucky to the west. In each instance the North managed to cultivate existing pro-Union sentiment and maintain control of divided states—if not all their citizens—through the use of an aggressive military presence and political arrests. And in addition to these successes, in August the western portion of Virginia broke off from the rest of the state and rejoined the Union.

While the border states were drawing the lion's share of the Union's political and military attention, much of the North was swept up in the war fervor. Throughout the Union word of the firing on Fort Sumter drew angry crowds into the streets in search of news and scapegoats. Citizens congregated in front of newspaper offices to read the latest reports. In Philadelphia mobs prowled the streets threatening supposed secessionists and demanding shows of patriotism. New York's Democratic Mayor Fernando Wood had been a strong advocate of conciliation with the South, going so far as to suggest that the city should declare its own independence in the midst of the crisis. But immediately after the firing began, Wood declared his patriotism and called on the city to fund the formation of Union regiments. After months of talking compromise, war enthusiasm had become the dominant sentiment. Most Northerners appeared eager to punish the rebels, and those who doubted the wisdom of war learned to keep their counsel.

In communities across the North, recruiting tents sprang up in a display of enthusiasm. While local dignitaries delivered patriotic pronouncements, glory-minded young men lined up to enlist. Even before Lincoln made his call, Northern governors had been busily assembling regiments for national service. The early patterns of enlistment reveal much about the world that embarked upon war. Although the call for volunteers came from the federal government, and the governors directed their states' efforts, the first companies were really formed from the bottom up. Often private citizens provided the impetus and even the funding for specific companies and regiments. Recruits vied to fill limited spaces in elite military companies; some unlucky ones offered cash rewards to anyone willing to relinquish a choice spot. Once formed, the volunteer regiments—each composed of ten hundred-man companies—offered themselves for state militia service; only the army regulars fought as United States troops. As long as there were more eager recruits than available spaces, state governors were most concerned with outfitting the volunteers and juggling competing bids for military commissions.

The composition of these first regiments mirrored the complex associational webs that characterized mid-nineteenth-century life. Small towns sent off entire groups of young men in just a few regiments. In the months and years that followed, letters from camp vividly portrayed the continuing importance of community ties as soldiers reported on the fates of cousins, in-laws, and boyhood friends. In larger cities recruits marched off to war as they had lived in peacetime: with co-workers or fellow students, as fire companies or ethnic groups, as neighbors or lifelong friends. The war did bring men of disparate backgrounds together

to fight side by side, but when new recruits paraded out of
town they often marched with the same men with whom
they had celebrated the most recent holiday.

The call to arms thrust the first wave of volunteers onto
center stage, both in the community at large and in a
thousand private dramas in homes, shops, and saloons, and
on streetcorners. Young men in their new military finery
adopted a proud swagger; friends who had not signed up
offered public congratulations, perhaps masking private jeal-
ousies. Any sunny afternoon that spring saw hordes of
Northerners making excursions to nearby military camps
where they watched the troops drill, returning home with
renewed confidence that the rebellion would soon be glor-
iously crushed. But if the untried troops dominated public
attention after Fort Sumter, from a more distant perspective
the frenzied months of mobilization are most remarkable
for the great breadth of participation, both in emotion and
in activity. Each enlistee engendered an array of highly
personal responses among his own loved ones. The events in
South Carolina coupled with the sweep of mobilization
broadened popular concern for national affairs. Northern
women seemed particularly changed by the experience, as
female diarists began filling their journals with detailed
accounts of distant events. In a more general sense the
outbreak of war jolted Americans—North and South—out
of their localistic sensibilities into contemplating heretofore
uninspected matters of "union," "nation," and the like. Still,
this enhanced national sense retained much of the traditional
focus on local concerns. In the years ahead, citizens on the
home front eagerly followed the course of the war, but they
saved their deepest interest for the activities of home-town
troops.

Many noncombatants were not satisfied merely to cheer
on the volunteers or pore over newspaper headlines. The
Fort Sumter crisis triggered a great many organized responses that revealed America's deep tradition of volunta-

rism, one largely different between men and women. While patriotic men worked in public—encouraging recruits, raising money to outfit regiments—Northern women gathered in thousands of drawing rooms to sew clothing for departing troops. As the conflict wore on, and both needs and skills evolved, home-front volunteers developed more sophisticated responses to the war's demands. But four years of carnage did not change certain basic truths. Much of the war effort relied on highly traditional, localized forms of voluntarism. And within those organizations men and women played equally important but quite different roles.

For the North's black women and men the outbreak of war signaled no clear change in status. Although Lincoln insisted that the war was for Union and not emancipation, most black and white abolitionists welcomed the conflict as a step in the right direction. But those black men who hoped to join the fight would have to wait nearly two years for that opportunity. In the first few months the North went to war to preserve the Union rather than to reshape its own society.

Through all the excitement and enthusiasm, the nation prepared for war with little organization or careful direction. Local quartermasters charged with outfitting the new troops found themselves in a near free-for-all as they competed for scarce military material. Most probably acted in good faith. But some savvy entrepreneurs calculated the changing market and charted a course to immediate war profits. In 1863 New York novelist Henry Morford published *The Days of Shoddy: A Novel of the Great Rebellion in 1861* to expose the evils committed by the North's "shoddy aristocracy," those businessmen who capitalized on the war enthusiasm by selling cheap merchandise at inflated prices. In one character, dry goods merchant Charles Holt, Morford combined the home front's worst evils. While other New Yorkers were swept up in the emotions of April 1861, Holt instructed his partner in Europe to buy up all available military cloth and to double their investment in cotton goods

"as cotton *must* rise under the new aspect of affairs."
Meanwhile, Holt's private life reinforced the reader's distaste
for his character. When the news from Fort Sumter arrived,
the merchant's young clerk felt overwhelmed with enthusiasm but hesitated to enlist for fear his wife would suffer in
his absence. The seemingly generous Holt volunteered to
continue the boy's salary in his absence and promised to
guarantee his family's protection if disaster fell. As soon as
the clerk was safely at the front, Holt launched a vigorous,
but of course unsuccessful, campaign to seduce the pretty
wife. In the novel's closing chapter, Morford exacts his
revenge against the nation's economic and moral enemies by
having Holt's head literally blown off by a sentry's bullet.

The riot in Baltimore, and Maryland's uncertain status, left
the capital at Washington temporarily isolated from the rest
of the Union. Even when the military secured control of
Maryland, the federal government remained precariously
close to the seat of war. Meanwhile, secession had entirely
recast Washington's political makeup. With the coming of
war many of the familiar points of debate became moot.
And the Democratic party lost much of its congressional
strength when its Southern members resigned their offices.
The war years certainly saw a continuation of some issues—
the future of slavery, for instance—under different guises,
but political battle lines were forever changed.

While the Republican party won the 1860 election with a
minority of the popular vote, Lincoln entered office as the
leader of a majority party. In addition to their objections to
the extension of slavery, the Republicans had come to stand
for a collection of economic policies—banking reform, protective tariffs, railroad land grants—that would enhance the
role of the federal government in promoting economic
growth. Such measures, some inherited from Whig predecessors, had met with resistance from Democrats of both

regions. Now the stage appeared set for new economic
policies that went beyond necessary war measures.

Abraham Lincoln brought many appealing personal qualities but little relevant experience to the White House. Other
than brief service fighting Indians during the Black Hawk
War, Lincoln had no military background. But from the
outset he evinced a strong belief in the indissolubility of the
Union, a conviction that he had the constitutional power to
direct the nation through the emergency, and a willingness
to exercise that power. Upon taking office the new president
declined to call Congress into special session, thus allowing
himself more room to operate while asserting the primacy of
the executive. His chief military goal, Lincoln announced,
was the preservation of the Union. Despite his own personal
distaste for slavery, Lincoln insisted he had no intention of
making war against the South's peculiar institution.

Given the critical role of the executive branch, Lincoln's
cabinet appointees were especially important. Rather than
select a group of personal admirers and bland functionaries,
he chose to surround himself with many of his party's
leading figures, including several who privately believed
they belonged in the White House. Two of the most important of those with presidential dreams were Secretary
of State William H. Seward and Treasury Secretary Salmon
P. Chase. Seward, who as governor of and senator from
New York had established himself as one of his party's
leading figures, tried to position himself as the power behind
the throne. The Ohioan Chase could barely keep his ambi-
tions in check. In his effort to cater to the North's vital
political regions, Lincoln named Pennsylvania power broker
Simon Cameron as secretary of war. Although Seward and
Chase periodically proved to be politically troublesome for
Lincoln, they also ran their departments with skill. But
Cameron never rose to the occasion, and Lincoln soon
banished him as ambassador to Russia. The remainder of
Lincoln's cabinet reflected a geographic cross section of the

North and border states. In Congress, as in the cabinet, Republicans distributed themselves along a broad political spectrum, but it took the strains of war to reveal their true differences. During the secession crisis Northern Democrats were more conciliatory toward the South, but they also rallied to the cause at the outbreak of war. When Lincoln delivered his Inaugural Address, Stephen Douglas, his former rival from Illinois, held the president's hat in an overt display of unity. But within months "the Little Giant" was dead, and soon portions of his party were in open dissent over the course of the war.

Before Congress convened in July, Lincoln announced several important initiatives apart from his call for three-month volunteers. From the outset he directed Treasury Secretary Chase to explore measures to fund the war effort. More important, on April 27 the new president served notice that he would use his war powers to the fullest when he ordered the suspension of the writ of habeas corpus—allowing arrests without charges—in selected areas in the North and border states. In Baltimore military officials threw suspected secessionists into Fort McHenry as part of the campaign to secure control of the state. For the next four years the administration walked a precarious path between the desire to protect civil liberties and the concern to quell dissent which might threaten the Union. And soon the Union adopted a number of other war measures—conscription, taxation, banking, emancipation—expanding the powers of the federal government. At each juncture Lincoln's opponents raised their voices in outrage, challenging his usurpation of power. But in that first summer most were willing to stand by the president.

Citizens' enthusiasm for the war was not initially matched by progress on the battlefield. As people on the home front clamored for action, armies on both sides drilled, maneuvered, and engaged in a few minor skirmishes. But as the summer of 1861 progressed, the Union's ninety-day enlistments wound down with most volunteers yet to see fighting. Finally, 37,000 Union soldiers under General Irvin McDowell engaged a Confederate force at Manassas Junction, the meeting point of two railroad lines outside Washington. Early reports declared a Union victory, but when Confederate reinforcements arrived, the green Northern troops broke and ran, scattering picnickers who had ventured from Washington to watch the decisive battle of the war.

For observers at home, the lessons of this First Battle of Bull Run were many. First, although both armies fought bravely at points, the engagement demonstrated that neither was properly prepared for serious conflict. While American observers recognized this, citizens on both sides felt outraged by the derisive reports of the battle filed by the London *Times*'s veteran military reporter, William Howard Russell. Second, each side realized that the other was deadly serious about the war. Victory would not come easily to either army. Finally, Northerners discovered that war was no place for picnics. After First Bull Run, both nations redoubled their commitment to the successful prosecution of the war.

2

Two Nations at War

As THE TROOPS straggled back to Washington following the Battle of Bull Run, Northerners took stock. This was
to be no brief adventure. The enemy to the South was not
merely a collection of hotheaded rebels, likely to cave in at
the first show of federal force. By the end of the summer of
1861, communities across the North had begun preparations
for a serious conflict.

To understand the Northern response, one must first
measure the two sides' material circumstances—wealth, industry, population—as they pertained to waging war, and
consider their cultural characteristics. The second need is to
keep in mind the military context. Many, though not all,
differences between the Northern and Southern home-front
experiences were dictated by military events and objectives.

In purely demographic terms the North entered the Civil
War with an enormous advantage. The free Union states had
a total population of 19 million; the eleven states of the
Confederacy totaled just over 9 million people. The slave
states that stayed with the Union—Delaware, Kentucky,
Maryland, and Missouri—added 3.2 million Northerners,
though that number included many Southern sympathizers
and Confederate volunteers. The total population figures
distort the true picture by including slaves and free blacks as
well as whites. How should we count the Confederacy's 3.5

million slaves in this comparison? On the one hand we must certainly reduce the South's eligible military manpower by that number; on the other hand, the availability of slave labor freed a larger share of Southern white men for military service. On the Northern side of the ledger we should consider the 179,000 black men—from both regions—who would eventually fight for the Union.

Best estimates indicate that the Confederacy had roughly a million white men of military age (between eighteen and forty-five) to draw on, whereas the North had three and a half times that number. These figures can also be tinkered with in various ways. Perhaps 100,000 men from the Northern border states fought for the Confederacy; but an estimated 45,000 white men from the upper South served on the Union side, and they were joined by an equal number of freed Confederate slaves. Moreover, although immigration in the United States dropped off with the secession crisis, it soon exceeded immediate prewar standards with roughly 800,000 immigrants arriving in the North during the war years, greatly augmenting the available work force and, to a lesser extent, providing more potential recruits.

In addition to its greater size, the Northern population was more diverse than its Southern counterpart. Only 392,000 (3.5 percent) Southerners were foreign-born in 1860, compared with 4 million (19.6 percent) in the rest of the country. Similarly, less then 10 percent of the Southern population and more than a quarter of the remainder of the nation lived in urban settings (2,500 or more people) on the eve of the war. Although the South was certainly the most racially mixed region, the disproportionate share of free blacks lived in the Union states. Only 132,000 free blacks lived in the Confederacy when the war began. A very similar number resided in the North's four slave states, and the free states held another 226,000 free blacks.

Throughout the first half of the nineteenth century the Northern United States had seen an extended period of

economic growth and development. Total output and per
capita output grew steadily as the manufacturing sector
expanded while agricultural productivity continued to swell.
Large factories emerged in some economic sectors, including
textiles, boots and shoes, and heavy machinery. As the
economy modernized, the North's financial systems and
transportation networks developed rapidly. The difference
in immigration and urbanization levels both reflected and
contributed to this process.

The Southern economy was far from moribund during
these antebellum decades. Built on a rising international
demand for cotton exports, total output and per capita
output in the South grew steadily. But investment in slaves
and land was at the expense of the sort of resource allocation
that had driven the free states' remarkable growth. Thus the
South grew without developing in the same directions or at
the same speed as the North. And much of its prosperity
depended on external demands for cotton and on ready
access to the Northern financial establishment.

Consequently, on the eve of the Civil War the North
enjoyed a number of economic advantages over its foe.
Roughly 90 percent of the nation's 1860 manufacturing
output had been from Northern states. The Confederacy
began the war with almost no functioning factories. In some
critical military-related sectors the Union's advantage was
greater still. The North produced seventeen times as much
cotton and woolen textiles as the South; thirty times as many
boots and shoes; twenty times as much pig iron; and
thirty-two times as many firearms. The Northern advantage
in transportation was enormous both in existing resources
and in capacity to expand. In 1860 there were twenty
thousand miles of railroad track in the Northern states,
twice the Confederate figure. The North also had twenty-
four times as many locomotives as well as a far superior
capacity to produce additional track and rolling stock. As
for water transportation, neither side had much of a navy—

about a dozen ships were available for immediate United States service when the war broke out—but the North had eleven times as many ships and boats as well as most of the nation's major shipyards. By the end of 1861 the federal navy boasted 260 warships, and many more were under construction.

To these advantages of quantity and capacity we must add the less measurable Northern superiority in mechanical skills. For decades Southern slaveowners had spoken disparagingly of the "greasy mechanics" of the Northern cities. Now the South had to scramble while its adversary could call on a large band of workers and entrepreneurs ready to focus their skills on a new set of problems. This advantage was vividly demonstrated shortly after Fort Sumter when troops from the 8th Massachusetts regiment arrived in Annapolis and found that rioters had destroyed most of the available rolling stock. Upon discovering a dilapidated old locomotive, a Massachusetts private volunteered, "That engine was made in our shop; I guess I can fit her up and run her." In the years that followed, the Confederacy performed quite well with its meager resources, but Union commanders repeatedly profited from the talents of their mechanics and from miracles performed by the Army Corps of Engineers.

With its clear manufacturing superiority, the North also bettered the South in agricultural capacity, particularly in the production of foodstuffs. In 1860, before the conflict's destruction had taken its toll on the Confederacy, the Northern states produced half the nation's corn, four-fifths of its wheat, and seven-eighths of its oats. When the war began the Union had nearly twice as many pack animals, and the Confederacy's available animals were disproportionately in the upper states where they were most liable to capture.

The powerful Northern economy gave the Union great advantages as it prepared for war. That abundance helped insulate Northerners from the economic hardships that the

Confederate home front later endured. The initial task for both sides was effectively to mobilize their available resources. Here too the North enjoyed several advantages. In addition to its private manufacturing base the Northern states had a well-developed market system supported by an extensive financial network. Where most Northerners at all economic levels were used to dealing in a cash market, large portions of the Southern agricultural sector continued to rely on subsistence farming or informal barter in addition to cash transactions. Those planters who grew staple crops for trade worked through international markets dominated by financial intermediaries from other regions. Compared with the North, the Confederacy lacked not only producers of military goods but the means for effectively distributing goods once produced. Similarly the North had both superior total wealth and a better financial structure to extract that wealth for national needs. In 1860 the states that would form the Confederacy had only 221 of the nation's 1,642 (13.4 percent) banks and branches. The North's chaotic banking system underwent important mid-war transformations, but from the outset the private financial sector provided an invaluable vehicle for war financing.

These measurable characteristics indicate that the North was both larger and more economically "modern" than its adversary, but the differences should not be overstated. The North of 1860 was far from the highly urbanized and industrialized world of later generations. In fact the vast majority of Americans in all regions lived in small towns or rural areas. Similarly the South was not simply a region of enormous, sprawling plantations. Fewer than a third of Confederate families owned any slaves at all on the eve of the war, and half of all slaveowners owned fewer than five slaves. Still, the worlds that clashed in 1861 had grown apart in ways that ran deeper than demographic characteristics and economic systems.

Most mid-nineteenth-century Americans felt their deepest ties with the local community rather than with the nation or even the state. Although we may marvel at the contemporary pace of economic growth and geographic expansion, change came slowly into individual lives. The country was still highly localistic and tradition-bound. And despite a variety of religious beliefs in some regions, it was an almost exclusively Christian—largely Protestant—world. Religious impulses had to share center stage with a fervent enthusiasm for the nation's history, replete with hallowed icons and ritual days. Perhaps nothing connected the North and South so strongly as a shared commitment to America's past. Each year communities across the land came together to celebrate Independence Day or to hear patriotic orations honoring George Washington's birthday. As the war began, one of the great oratorical challenges on both sides was to establish rightful claim to that heroic tradition.

Each region had a clear and essentially similar system of inequality. By 1860 most Northern states had eliminated slavery, but nowhere did African Americans enjoy legal, political, or economic equality with whites. An equally immutable, if not quite as crippling, set of inequalities separated men and women in both the North and the South. Although they watched the 1860 election returns with interest, American women had no official voice in the political process—they were not allowed to vote. Antebellum women, especially in the North, had various means of influencing the course of public events, but it was the extraordinary woman who enjoyed the opportunity to speak in public.

The economies of the North and the South were fundamentally different, with much of the Southern agricultural system built upon slave labor, but economic inequalities in both regions were marked. In the South access to political and economic power was largely limited to a landed elite, who also exerted a tremendous cultural control over their worlds. Avenues to upward mobility were slightly more open in the North, but like their Southern counterparts, the richest few percent of all Northerners owned an enormous share of the nation's wealth. And access to those top rungs on the economic ladder remained limited.

Citizens on both sides of the Mason-Dixon line also shared a strong tradition of political participation. In 1860 more than 80 percent of the North's eligible voters and nearly 70 percent of Southerners went to the polls. Adherence to political parties was particularly powerful, often built on deeply felt community issues and an intense loyalty to local party organizations. In all regions, but especially in the Northeast, party leadership fostered fierce partisanship through energetic political clubs, bands, and torchlight processions. These party ties were national or—in the case of the Republican party—at least regional, but Americans' localistic worldview was mirrored by the structure of antebellum government. Average citizens had little contact with the federal government in the first half of the nineteenth century. Most national political attention was focused on foreign affairs, the unorganized territories, and debates over economic policies. In 1860 the total federal budget was only about $63 million. At mid-century the entire nonmilitary federal bureaucracy contained only twenty thousand employees. The government collected no national income tax and took on little responsibility for the social or economic welfare of individual citizens.

Although the populations of both regions were quite homogeneous by modern standards, the North had larger proportions of immigrants and free blacks. This diversity helped mold regional associational patterns. In Northern cities where immigrants were most numerous, fire companies, saloons, and clubs organized along ethnic and religious lines. Forced geographic and occupational separation helped create autonomous black enclaves within some communities. Such racial and ethnic allegiances remained crucial when the war came.

The unpleasant side of this associational impulse—collective violence—was powerful both in the antebellum decades and into the war years. The Jacksonian era (1829–1837) has been characterized as one of the most violent periods in American history. By most objective standards the antebellum South was the nation's most violent, militaristic region, but the periodic outbursts of rioting that punctuated the 1830s and 1840s were largely centered in Northern cities and towns. The clashes took various forms, reflecting the array of social and political tensions accompanying Northern development. In some emerging industries organized workers battled employers over wages or changing work conditions. Wherever immigrants clustered in substantial numbers they risked hostility from the host population or from other immigrant groups. Sometimes the violence took on a religious aspect, as when established Protestants battled newly arrived Irish Catholics. The worst of the antebellum riots were not over ethnicity but race. As the nation debated the future of Southern slavery, angry Northern mobs repeatedly attacked abolitionist leaders and, in much bloodier episodes, free blacks. One of the North's great challenges of the war years was to harness the strengths of a society built upon distinctive communities without imploding under the strain of ethnic and racial hostility.

The evangelical religious impulses that swept through England and the United States in the second quarter of the century left their deepest mark on the more rapidly transforming North. One outgrowth of this renewed religiosity was a rejection of the remaining strands of Calvinism in favor of a faith in the inherent perfectibility of humankind. These ideas, coupled with the North's economic modernization, spawned a number of institutional developments that further separated it from its Southern neighbor. Cities and states tackled the challenges of crime, poverty, sickness, and insanity with renewed vigor, if only modest success. Asylums sprang up throughout the North as reformers sought to apply principles of organization, logic, and restraint to the nation's social ills. This institutional experience, too, played a role in the Union's approach to the war.

The impulses that launched hundreds of asylums also led thousands of Northerners to throw themselves into associations bent on reforming antebellum behavior. The litany of mid-nineteenth-century reform movements is quite long, ranging from Sylvester Graham's bizarre teachings on diet and sex to the large and extremely powerful Temperance Movement. Among these many efforts, abolitionism ranks as the most important antebellum reform movement. As the abolitionist movement gained momentum in the 1830s and 1840s, its adherents split over goals and methods, but the competing groups shared a commitment to grassroots mobilization. Taken together the various antebellum benevolent and reform movements taught Northerners important lessons about organizing and financing voluntary activities. When the war came these familiar efforts provided an important template for new kinds of voluntarism.

One of the best comparative measures of a society's priorities is its attention to education. Generally speaking, resources devoted to educating children are at the expense of short-term economic needs (schools cost money and students could be working) in the interest of broader social and economic goals. The free population of the United States on the eve of the Civil War was quite well educated. At mid-century the national literacy rate (excluding slaves) was nearly 90 percent. The literacy rate for free Southerners was 83 percent, a high figure but below the 94 percent literacy of the free states and New England's extraordinary 98.5 percent. The Northeastern states had long led the rest of the country in public school systems. As early as 1830 nearly three-fourths of school-age children in New England and New York attended public schools. In 1852 Massachusetts passed the nation's first compulsory education law. By 1860 roughly 75 percent of Northern children between ages five and sixteen were in school, compared with roughly 35 percent in the South. And those Northern children who were in school attended more days each year than their Southern counterparts.

The impulse to educate children reflected a desire for an educated population and work force and a belief that schools were an efficient means of social control—they kept unruly children off the streets. One result of a well-educated population was that Northerners had access to a wider spectrum of information. Thanks partly to the dramatic reduction in printing costs, the nineteenth century had witnessed an explosion in the number of cheap newspapers, particularly in Northern cities. In 1860 the North published three times as many copies of newspapers per capita as the South. The free states were also well ahead of the South in book publishing, book sales, and similar literary indices.

Thus Northerners in general, and Northeasterners in particular, likely saw their local worlds in the context of news from a much wider arena. This expanding worldview moved alongside an enlarged market orientation in which local businesses were becoming increasingly tied to events in distant ports. This may have helped them contemplate the abstract notion of "nationalism" that was at the core of the Union's war effort. Similarly, exposure to different worlds and ideas left Northerners relatively more open to a changing society. Receptivity to change proved important to both sides as they adjusted to the war's demands. Still, while some citizens were developing a cosmopolitan worldview, most Northerners remained localistic and traditional in their perspective, except perhaps when compared with their Southern brethren.

Among the Union's advantages going into the Civil War, presumably its superior military establishment would rank near the top. After all, the Confederacy was an upstart country fighting against an established nation that had defeated Mexico just over a decade earlier. But in fact the United States Army was hopelessly unprepared to embark on a major war when Fort Sumter fell. At the time the federal army numbered only sixteen thousand men, most of them stationed in the West to battle American Indians. Seven of the Army bureau heads had been in uniform since the War of 1812.

Although the Confederacy was forced to build an army from scratch, it could draw on the fighting skills of a highly militaristic populace. When the country appeared on the verge of war, rebel editorialists reacted with confidence, insisting that an agrarian nation of hunters and horsemen could easily defeat any number of greasy mechanics. Each Southern community boasted at least one private militia company commanded by men from the local elite. When the United States fought Mexico in the 1840s it was largely at the instigation of expansionist Southerners, and the volunteers for that conflict came disproportionately from the slave states. The South also enjoyed a head start in wartime recruiting. As noted earlier, immediately after the seceding states formed the Confederacy, Jefferson Davis called for the recruitment of a 100,000-man army. And as soon as war began in earnest, a third of the nation's West Point graduates gave up their commissions to join the Confederacy, giving the rebels an important core of experienced military leaders.

Comparing the strengths and characteristics of the two sides, it is worth noting that the Union and the Confederacy did not approach the Civil War with identical objectives. Certainly both sides hoped to "win" the war, but winning a war can mean very different things to different peoples. During the American Civil War the differing circumstances facing the two nations had a great impact on how home-front citizens experienced the conflict.

The Confederacy entered the Civil War hoping simply to survive as an independent nation. It had no need to overwhelm its antagonists or even to conquer territory. As Jefferson Davis declared, "All we ask is to be left alone." In strategic terms, Southerners could have pursued various routes to that end. Had they elected to dig in and conduct a defensive war, they could have conserved resources and placed the burden of attack on the North. Historically, outnumbered nations have often survived against military powers by making the price of victory too heavy. But such a strategy would have had other costs for the South. First, a critical Southern goal was to achieve international recognition. Military passivity would not help Southerners demonstrate their viability. More important, Confederate morale required victories, not simply survival.

The Union Army, on the other hand, had to adopt strategies that would lead to Confederate surrender. The Southern economy had long depended on international trade. If the North could "strangle" its adversary with an effective blockade, perhaps it could force it into submission. But even while pursuing this strategy, the North would have to find ways to take the war to the enemy.

These different military objectives helped offset the Confederacy's great numerical disadvantages. West Point–trained strategists learned that it took roughly three times as many men and resources to attack as to defend; this was almost exactly equal to the advantage enjoyed by the North. But no war is merely about numbers. The differing objectives of the Confederacy and the Union gave each quite distinct psychological and ideological challenges. White Southerners went to war to defend their homes and their ways of life against the challenge by the North. Such goals were concrete and powerful. The Union, in contrast, had to maintain support for the war with a more amorphous set of goals. In the spring of 1861 the North rose to the call to arms partly out of a spirit of vengeance against the traitorous South. But as the nation dug in for the long haul, its leaders had to rally support for the abstract goal of preserving the Union. Such an objective certainly lacked the visceral appeal of the Confederacy's war aims. For some Northerners the war, despite the president's insistence to the contrary, was really about slavery, thus elevating the conflict to a higher plane. At mid-war the nation's official stance changed with Lincoln's Emancipation Proclamation. This shift spurred some citizens to more enthusiastic patriotism while leading others to turn their backs on the cause.

Although the defense of hearth and home proved a powerful appeal to Confederate men and women, the years of war took a heavier toll on the Southern home front. Confederate soldiers had to contend with the knowledge that their loved ones were suffering through economic shortages and the threat of enemy invasion. In contrast, the Union economy prospered through most of the war, and only small pockets of federal territory ever saw enemy troops. This suggests yet another link between the war's military history and circumstances on the home front.

The most important connection between the home front and the war effort centered on each side's mobilization efforts. The South was far more successful in getting a high proportion of eligible men into uniform. Certainly the depths of wartime passion were instrumental in this success. But both nations also had to devise means to provide material support for their armies. Here the North's advantage went beyond its greater wealth and tremendous industrial superiority. The Confederacy not only lacked an established manufacturing sector, its localized economy and immature market system were poorly suited for mass mobilization. Moreover, when the Southern states seceded from the Union they waved the banner of states' rights, as they had for decades in national political debates. Suddenly, with the formation of the Confederacy, the same men who had defended state autonomy against the encroachment of central authority found themselves in the middle of a major war. Such a war forced both governments to expand their powers, sometimes at the expense of individual freedoms. Some war measures raised opposition in both the North and the South, but the Confederate administration faced the tougher challenge in trying to construct a strong central administration in the face of such traditional hostility.

PART TWO

How a Free People Conduct
a Long War
July 1861 to Late 1863

IN THE FIRST weeks and months after the firing on Fort
Sumter, Northerners threw themselves into a number of
emergency measures to fill the ranks, outfit the troops, and
generally support the war effort. Hundreds of committees
formed to carve out areas of involvement. With this remarkable show of energy came quite a bit of chaos. By mid-
summer the first enlistments had expired and the Battle of
Bull Run had offered some hint of what was to come.

In late 1862, frustrated with national debates over public
policy, Philadelphian Charles Janeway Stillé published a
pamphlet, *How a Free People Conduct a Long War*. Stillé's
own ideas were quite explicit on the matter (he drew on
England's experience during the Napoleonic Wars for his
model), but in a larger sense this was exactly what the
Union had to sort out over the two years following Bull
Run. As a "free people," individual Northerners claimed
certain rights and responsibilities in the prosecution of the
Civil War. And as it became clear this would be a long war,
the role of those at home became progressively important,
and more and more difficult.

Northerners made a number of adjustments on the home
front between the summer of 1861 and late 1863, as the

nation shifted from ad hoc measures to a more formally organized war effort. These adjustments occurred at all levels of society: national, state and local, familial and individual.

3

Military and Political Adjustments

IN BOTH CONCRETE and abstract senses, Americans had to "learn" how to fight the Civil War. Little in their past or in the history of other nations provided much of a guide. The man faced with the most difficult lessons, and the shortest time to learn them, was Abraham Lincoln. The lanky man from Illinois knew almost nothing of military strategy and little more of national politics. In both areas he found many people anxious to guide his thinking.

The military history of the Civil War from July 1861 through the Fall of 1863 is extraordinarily complex, dotted with the names of dozens of major battles and hundreds of flamboyant heroes. But overall, several key patterns emerge. In these two years most of the war was fought in three theaters: the West, primarily Tennessee, Kentucky, and Mississippi; the East, either between the two capitals of Washington and Richmond, or twice when the Confederacy invaded the North; and along the Confederacy's 3,500-mile coastline. Although the Eastern theater was the site of a dozen famous battles, none of these engagements yielded a conclusive result. That is, after more than two years of war neither side had captured substantial territory, and the competing armies were always able to leave the field unmolested. In the process a frustrated Lincoln worked his way through most of the Union's leading generals in search of a man who could lead the federal forces to victory. Yet Union generals in the West—maneuvering out of the eye of the Eastern urban press—achieved several important victories, culminating in the seizure of Vicksburg, Mississippi. Meanwhile, the North's navy established its superiority along the coasts, in various river campaigns, and on the high seas.

In the Western theater the Union's principal objectives were to solidify control over the border states of Kentucky, Tennessee, and Missouri, and to hold sway over the western river system, the Confederacy's lifeline to the southwestern states. The first major Union victories in the West, and the first major reasons to celebrate throughout the North, came in February 1862 when Brigadier General Ulysses S. Grant captured Forts Henry and Donelson in Tennessee. From there Grant moved south down the Tennessee River, two months later fighting the bloody battle of Shiloh. That winter Grant began his campaign against Vicksburg, the Confederate stronghold on the Mississippi River. In the meantime the Union Navy, under Admiral David Farragut, was intent on securing control over the southern portion of the Mississippi. On April 25 Farragut captured New Orleans at the mouth of the river. From there he began his push up the Mississippi where, like Grant, his ultimate target was Vicksburg.

In the East Lincoln reacted to the First Battle of Bull Run with two successive calls for 500,000 three-year volunteers. Unhappy with McDowell's performance at Bull Run, the president named thirty-four-year-old George B. McClellan to command the newly formed Army of the Potomac. In the months to come the popular McClellan proved to be a masterful military architect, building a huge, well-drilled army out of hordes of raw recruits. But as autumn gave way to winter McClellan repeatedly resisted calls to send his army into action. Finally in March he launched his Peninsular Campaign. McClellan's plan was to land his army on the coast about fifty miles southeast of Richmond and march up the Virginia peninsula to capture the Confederate capital. The army's way had been paved by the victory of the *Monitor* over the *Merrimack* in the famed clash of ironclad ships at Hampton Roads, at the mouth of the Chesapeake River. On May 31 the rebels finally engaged Union troops east of Richmond. In June McClellan battled the Army of Northern Virginia, under its newly appointed commander Robert E. Lee, only to be driven back following a series of spectacular battles.

After the failure of the Peninsular Campaign, Lincoln called Henry Halleck east in July to serve as general-in-chief and gave John Pope command of fifty thousand men stationed north of Richmond. As soon as Lee saw McClellan in retreat, he sent Stonewall Jackson north to threaten Pope. In late August the Confederate Army cornered Pope at the Second Battle of Bull Run, forcing his retreat to the defenses at Washington. Lee made a daring decision, choosing to cross the Potomac and invade Maryland, with Harrisburg, Pennsylvania, as his ultimate objective. During the frenzied days before the battle, McClellan had refused to hurry to Pope's aid. Lincoln later termed that behavior "unpardonable," but he nonetheless returned Pope's defeated army to the Army of the Potomac with McClellan once again in command. As Lee moved North, McClellan set out after him with Lincoln's order to "destroy the Rebel Army if possible." That goal seemed well within reach when one of McClellan's men stumbled upon a copy of Lee's orders which revealed that he had once again split his army. McClellan engaged Lee in mid-October near Antietam Creek in western Maryland. The Battle of Antietam proved to be the bloodiest single day of the war. After several Northern attacks, the struggle ended in stalemate with more than 26,000 casualties. Although the Union had far superior numbers, Lee managed to maintain his position until night-fall with the support of A. P. Hill's troops who arrived on the scene late in the afternoon. The next morning the Confederate troops slipped away.

McClellan's failure to press his advantage infuriated Lincoln, who had been hoping for a major victory as an occasion to announce a dramatic new policy toward slavery. Despite his frustration the president used the occasion of Lee's retreat to issue his preliminary Emancipation Proclamation, declaring that on the 1st of the year all slaves in states still under rebellion would be free. Meanwhile, in the West the Confederate General Braxton Bragg matched Lee's invasion with a raid of his own from Tennessee into Kentucky. As in the East, the Union Army, commanded by Don Carlos Buell, managed to stop the invasion, defeating Bragg at Perryville, Kentucky, on October 8, but without pressing the advantage. A few weeks later Buell gave way to Major General William S. Rosecrans.

As the winter of 1862–1863 began the Union Army had made substantial progress at both ends of the Mississippi and had established control over Missouri, Kentucky, western Tennessee, and West Virginia. But much to Lincoln's chagrin, a series of Eastern generals had failed to subdue Lee's outnumbered Army of Northern Virginia. Meanwhile, the Union Navy had established a stranglehold on Confederate shipping while successfully winning several important footholds on the Southern coastline.

By November the president had lost patience with McClellan's excuses and replaced him with Ambrose Burnside. Burnside's opportunity came the next month when he faced Lee at Fredericksburg, Virginia. But once again Lee escaped as the Union suffered twelve thousand casualties in one day's fighting. Lincoln then turned to "Fighting Joe" Hooker to command his army in the East. Hooker waited out the winter and in April undertook a flanking maneuver against Lee. But with brilliant tactics Lee managed to defeat Hooker at the Battle of Chancellorsville though he had only half as many men available. For the Confederacy the victory was bittersweet: General Stonewall Jackson was accidentally killed by one of his own pickets.

That June Lee again threw Northeasterners into a panic by launching another invasion up the Shenandoah Valley. Hooker trailed his adversary, intent on a return engagement, but Lincoln once more changed commanders, this time selecting General George Meade. On July 1 detachments from both armies met at the small town of Gettysburg, Pennsylvania. Over the next three days the two armies battled along a "fishhook" of hills south and west of the town. Of the many famed moments in the Battle of Gettysburg, the most dramatic—and tragic—was Pickett's Charge on the third day. This infantry charge, in which more than 10,000 rebel soldiers marched across open fields into Union artillery fire, ended in hideous failure. By the close of the third day the federal troops had lost 23,000 of 85,000 men, and the Confederates had more than 20,000 casualties from their original 65,000. But Meade, like McClellan before him, failed to press his advantage and let the defeated Lee escape South.

As citizens throughout the North celebrated the glorious news of Lee's defeat, their jubilation was doubled by word that Vicksburg had finally surrendered to Grant on Independence Day. This victory ended months of failed efforts and a relentless six-week siege of the Confederate stronghold on the Mississippi. But despite these two crucial triumphs, it was nearly two more years before the Confederacy finally surrendered.

The political challenges posed by the Civil War weighed heavy on both national governments. Some of these challenges, as Charles Stillé implied, were common to any democratic government engaged in a military conflict. Others were peculiar to civil wars in which brothers literally take up arms against each other. And still other wartime chal-

lenges reflected the specific political makeup of the competing nations.

When a democracy goes to war it must come to terms
with two distinct sets of political questions. First, who will
have the power necessary to prosecute the war, and how
much power is that? The Constitution was constructed with
a careful balance of powers among the three branches. The
founders gave the executive branch its greatest autonomy in
conducting foreign policy, where a lengthy legislative process can become unwieldy. Nonetheless, the Lincoln administration quickly found itself in unmapped territory as it
organized to fight the Civil War. A related set of dilemmas
concern individual freedoms. What does a nation dedicated
to free speech and an independent press do when open
dissent apparently threatens to undermine the war effort?
These questions framed much of the formal political debate
in the war's first years.

The party structure in the North—and the absence of a
party system in the South—played a vital role in shaping
political debate throughout the conflict. With the outbreak
of war, leaders in both parties had called for an end to
partisan politics. But after the failure at Bull Run the North
returned to a more defined two-party system. The Republican leadership was a diverse, independent-minded group.
The very newness of the party ensured that each member
had gone through a personal political odyssey before becoming a Republican. Once the war was underway these men
stretched out along an ideological spectrum from so-called
Radical Republicans—who insisted from the outset that the
war should be fought for emancipation—to more moderate
and conservative voices. These divisions were neither formally structured nor consistent across all issues, but Lincoln
always had to contend with party members to his left and
right as well as an emerging resistance from the Democratic
party. And, to add to his difficulties, he had filled his
cabinet with some of the party's most ambitious men.

When mobilization for war began, Lincoln took the initiative from the legislative branch by refusing to call Congress into special session. By the time Congress convened on July 4 they were faced with the task of either ratifying or undoing the president's early actions. With the Southern representatives absent, Republicans dominated the Senate with 31 members, as opposed to only 10 Democrats and 8 Constitutional Unionists. In the House the numbers were similar: 105 Republican representatives enjoyed a substantial majority over 43 Democrats and 30 Unionists. After decades of political stalemate, the removal of obstructionist Southerners left the Republicans well situated to enact their legislative agenda. But they also found themselves without many established leaders in both houses. In the House, Pennsylvania's Radical Republican Thaddeus Stevens quickly moved to the fore as the chair of the powerful Ways and Means Committee. But the Senate, long home for the nation's most brilliant political leaders, had lost valuable experience to the Confederacy and to Lincoln's cabinet. More damaging still, Stephen A. Douglas, the leading Northern Democrat, died in June after vowing to subordinate all party differences to the war effort.

By the time Congress met in special session, most of the agenda for the next four years had been set. Militarily the crucial issues involved the raising of men and the direction of the army. At the Treasury Salmon P. Chase was experimenting with various means to raise funds and finance the war effort. On the home front the suspension of the writ of habeas corpus and waves of political arrests had already sparked controversy. Meanwhile, abolitionists in and out of Congress pressured Lincoln to turn the war into a crusade against slavery.

When Congress gathered on Independence Day, Abraham Lincoln launched the special session by defending his actions —particularly the militia call-up and the suspension of the writ of habeas corpus—to that point, and by asking Congress to provide 400,000 more men and $400 million to supply them. Essentially he dared Congress to undo what he had already done while challenging them to provide the means to maintain the nation on the course he had already set. In the next twenty-nine days Congress gave the president what he wanted. Where Lincoln had sought 400,000 men, they authorized half a million. The House appropriated the requested funds with bipartisan support. Throughout that month Washington rang with patriotic rhetoric, calling for party politics to be set aside. In the midst of the session the two armies met at Bull Run. Several congressmen were on hand to witness the Union's first major loss; they returned to their work with a renewed commitment to the war effort. But even in their dedication there were seeds of future conflict, as Congress refused formal approval of the suspension of the writ of habeas corpus.

When the 37th Congress reconvened in December 1861 for its first long session, some of the blind enthusiasm of that summer had already waned and the major points of political conflict had begun to emerge. As would remain the case throughout the war, the national mood reflected progress on the battlefield. For months George McClellan had been drilling his troops while refusing to engage the enemy. In Washington congressmen chafed at this inactivity while Radical Republicans questioned the wisdom of leaving the Army of the Potomac in the hands of an avowed Democrat. As dissatisfaction grew, both houses debated resolutions calling for more open attacks on slavery and questioning the military handling of the war. Still, patriotic enthusiasm prevailed. Those who called for negotiated peace could find little support. And both houses voted to expel several disloyal members from the border states.

Meanwhile, Treasury Secretary Chase was overseeing an economic crisis which revealed the depths of the war's challenge to established practices. As a legacy of Jacksonian politics, the federal government's finances remained totally separate from the nation's byzantine system of private banks. All dealings with the government were in specie—hard coin—rather than in bank notes. Moreover, the nation's Treasury had traditionally relied on tariffs and land sales, rather than direct taxation, to fund its activities. Such practices had been reasonable in the antebellum decade when the national budget had averaged less than 2 percent of the gross national product. Faced with the enormous costs of war, Chase determined they should be financed by borrowing, through the sale of bonds. But by clinging to its insistence on payment in specie, the government precipitated a financial crisis. On December 30 the nation's banks and the Treasury suspended specie payments, and the North seemed on the verge of financial collapse. These economic issues found their way into the 37th Congress through various routes, many ending up in Thaddeus Stevens's House Ways and Means Committee. In the special session Congress had passed a modest, but still quite revolutionary, tax package. That January Congress debated a series of responses to the specie crisis. On February 25 it passed the Legal Tender Act, authorizing the Treasury to issue $150 million in notes, known as greenbacks, not backed by specie. The measure saved the day for the Union economy, but not without clamorous controversy.

That summer, as the flow of willing recruits dwindled, Congress debated another set of measures that would take the federal government onto unfamiliar terrain. Its ultimate solution, the July 1862 Militia Act, was a modest step toward national conscription legislation. The Militia Act authorized the president to call out the militia for nine months, with quotas to be distributed to the states. The legislation established broad parameters for recruiting but left the actual process in the hands of the states. It also opened the door for more aggressive federal action by allowing the president to act if the states proved ineffectual. With the Militia Act, as with the earlier financial legislation, Congress had responded to military necessity by gradually enhancing the power of the national state.

While the 37th Congress devoted much of its first full session to giving Lincoln the tools to wage war, it also began to assert its right to a larger say in how the war was waged. Congress's Joint Committee on the Conduct of the War became the crucial means by which the legislative branch claimed a voice in directing the military effort. Formed as a committee of inquiry in response to the Battle of Balls Bluff, the seven-man committee went on to investigate unpopular military appointments, charges of official corruption, and questions of military strategy and organization. It became the best-known wartime congressional committee, but in fact Congress exercised its investigatory power throughout the war through thirty-five select and standing committees.

Lincoln was also at odds with members of Congress over his administration's occasionally cavalier approach to civil liberties. Under William Seward, State Department officials had enthusiastically exercised the power to make political arrests, prompting Lyman Trumbull, chair of the Senate Judiciary Committee, to introduce resolutions calling on Secretary Seward to explain his actions. Lincoln finally responded to criticism by curtailing the power to arrest and shifting it to the War Department. Still, conflicts over arbitrary arrests persisted.

By the autumn of 1862 Abraham Lincoln found himself confronting an intricate political puzzle. In Congress and in his own cabinet he heard radical voices calling for a more aggressive policy toward the rebels, with the abolition of slavery as the ultimate objective. But he also had to reckon with a growing portion of the national electorate that was dissatisfied with the progress of military events and unsure about some of the measures passed in the name of war. The accumulated weight of political arrests, greenbacks, protective tariffs, military incompetence, and militia drafts had driven increasing numbers into the ranks of the Democrats. On the issue of slavery Lincoln had continued to steer a moderate course, fearing that if he turned the Union forces into an army of liberation he would lose valuable support in the North and potential allies in the South. But on September 22 the president unveiled his preliminary Emancipation Proclamation, announcing his plan to issue the formal proclamation on the 1st of the year. Although not as radical as some would have liked, the proclamation dramatically changed the war's essential character, prompting a complex combination of jubilant celebration and angry dissent.

The Democratic party, like the Republican, was no monolithic institution. As the conflict entered its second year the Democrats began to split. Prowar Democrats remained staunchly loyal to the cause while decrying those measures which they claimed expanded federal powers in violation of the Constitution. But others broke ranks and began calling for an end to the war. Republican newspapers labeled the most vocal peace Democrats "Copperheads," after the poisonous snake. The Copperheads deftly turned the insult into a symbol of pride by wearing copper Liberty Head pennies on their lapels. While many in the North called them traitors, the Copperheads claimed they were true patriots as they rallied around the slogan, "The Constitution as it is, the Union as it was." At their head stood flamboyant Ohio Congressman Clement L. Vallandigham, who had called for a negotiated peace from the outset. When the war measures mounted he openly assailed Lincoln's usurpations of power.

As 1862 drew to a close, most Northern states braced for elections that would serve as referenda on the Republicans' administration of the war and on Lincoln's planned Emancipation Proclamation. The party in power often loses ground in off-year elections, when there is no presidential vote, but when the nation is at war voters tend to rally around the flag and thus the current administration. In 1862 the Democrats won a number of striking victories. They gained thirty-two seats in the House, mostly in Pennsylvania, New Jersey, New York, Ohio, Indiana, and Illinois. New York and New Jersey elected Democratic governors. In Indiana and Illinois, Lincoln's home turf, the opposition party won control of the state legislatures. And even where Republicans maintained control, Democrats generally fared better than they had in 1860.

The 1862 results indicate important pockets of dissatisfaction with the war and particularly with the plan for emancipation. Nonetheless the Republicans carried New England and the upper North as well as the border states (with the help of federal troops who intimidated pro-South voters). Although the margin had narrowed, Republicans still held a majority in the House; in the Senate they actually enjoyed a net gain of five seats. Those Republican congressmen who remained had added incentive to close ranks in the spirit of party unity. Nevertheless, the key to future political success would be the events on the battlefield.

When Congress met in December 1862 for its lame-duck session, the furor over Lincoln's emancipation proposal dominated political discourse. In his second annual message the President proposed a series of constitutional amendments to ease emancipation by compensating slaveowners for their losses and funding the distant colonization of freed slaves. Compensated emancipation and colonization had been dear to Lincoln's heart for some time, but these measures, like his earlier proposals, failed to win sufficient support.

Faced with military and electoral reverses, and frustrated by the president's gradual approach to emancipation, Republican senators gathered on December 16 to flex their political muscle. The caucus sent a delegation to meet with Lincoln two days later, and in a three-hour meeting called for a more rigorous prosecution of the war, an enlarged decision-making role for the cabinet, and the appointment of more assertive cabinet members. The subtext for these latter demands soon became clear. Secretary Chase had been complaining to his radical allies that Seward was influencing the president in wrong directions. Seward knew of the planned assault and had already tendered his resignation, which Lincoln had yet to accept. Lincoln managed the affair marvelously. He arranged a meeting between the delegation and the cabinet, without Seward. The senators were shocked to discover that the other cabinet members denied Chase's claims. Chase, embarrassed by the proceedings, offered his own resignation. Lincoln declared that he would keep both his invaluable secretaries on hand while maintaining their resignations on file in case either strayed. In so doing he reasserted his superiority over the cabinet and the Senate without losing the services of either Chase or Seward.

In the first months of 1863, while Grant was trying to pry the rebels loose from Vicksburg in the West and Lee was outmaneuvering a succession of Union generals in the East, Congress enacted critical legislation on manpower, finance, and civil liberties, three central areas of political debate. With the number of military recruits dwindling, it passed the Enrollment Act, setting up machinery for a federal draft. In response to the call for a stable currency and a coherent banking structure, it enacted the National Banking Act. And as an answer to the continuing controversy over political arrests, Congress issued the Habeas Corpus Act, which sought to place curbs on the actions of the secretaries of war and state while asserting its own constitutional right to a say in the matter.

In one sense the new legislature continued to act to give Lincoln the tools of war that he requested. At the same time its actions further enlarged the powers of the federal government. In this sense the war's first years had a clear nationalizing impact. Moreover, Congress succeeded in reasserting its own role vis-à-vis Abraham Lincoln and the executive branch.

The 37th Congress also found time to pass a series of laws

that had no direct connection with the war effort but served to promote the Republicans' 1860 platform. The Homestead Act provided that loyal heads of households would, on application, receive 160 acres of federal land in the Midwest. Congress followed this with the Pacific Railroad Bill which granted sections of public land to railroad companies laying track to the west. Both bills had been part of the party's national platform. These measures, combined with legislation on tariffs and banking, reflected the newfound power of the Republican party.

When the 37th Congress adjourned on March 4, 1863, the Union's military effort was going badly, and the nation was suffering from a number of political conflicts. By that summer the Democrats enjoyed growing support throughout the Union. Popular frustration with slow military progress fueled this support, but clearly the Democratic message held particular appeal to voters in some areas. The strongest Democratic base, and many of the loudest Copperhead voices, came out of the Midwest states of Ohio, Indiana, and Illinois. There the party built upon long-felt antagonisms to the economic and cultural power of the East. In many cases Republican war legislation appeared merely to be enacting an agenda of expanded national government which the heirs to Jefferson and Jackson felt compelled to resist. In addition to distrusting Eastern commercial interests, Midwestern Democrats shared a vehement racism. The specter of emancipation, and a flood of free blacks moving into their communities, triggered intense negrophobic reactions in speeches and editorials throughout the region. Finally, Democratic party organizations in the Midwest were strengthened by ethnic ties which became intertwined with party loyalty. Although it did not retain their passionate nativism, the Republican party had absorbed most of the old Know Nothings, whereas the Democrats had long been the party of immigrants. This connection was only reinforced by the

Emancipation Proclamation, which was especially controversial among some ethnic groups.

The Copperheads also enjoyed strong support in major urban areas where ethnic tensions combined with class antagonisms to create a vehement hostility to emancipation. New York, with its large Irish population, was a center of disaffection. In the decades before the war working-class New Yorkers had rioted repeatedly against free blacks, whom they saw as illegitimate labor competition. The twin forces of conscription and emancipation triggered more wartime racial violence. In 1860 Democrat Fernando Wood was mayor of New York City; two years later he moved on to become an outspoken Copperhead congressman. Philadelphia, a Northern city with strong social and economic ties to the South, also became an important haven for peace Democrat sentiment. Although Lincoln's supporters carried the city in both 1860 and 1864, their victories owed much to playing down racial issues in favor of local economic concerns.

For the Democrats the 1862 elections and their aftermath witnessed the emergence of new leaders. Horatio Seymour, New York's newly elected governor, became his party's most prominent officeholder. In his inaugural address he maintained his support for the war but assailed Lincoln for his emancipation policy. Later the New York Democrat attacked federal conscription legislation and illegal political arrests, including that of Clement Vallandigham. Vallandigham actually lost his Ohio congressional seat in 1862, but he continued to be a leading voice among radical Copperheads.

If Horatio Seymour emerged as the spokesman of the political opposition, and Clement Vallandigham remained its volatile lightning rod, the true favorite of the Democrats was George B. McClellan. As commander of the Army of the Potomac the young West Point graduate had fallen from Lincoln's graces with his endless excuses, arrogance, and finger-pointing. Even when his military stock was high,

McClellan's outspoken allegiance to the Democrats had worried Republicans. In July 1862, while in camp at Harrison's Landing, Virginia, McClellan summarized his grand military and political strategy in an audacious memo to Lincoln, in which he stressed that the war must be fought with no damage to the Constitution. Specifically, "military arrests should not be tolerated," private property should be protected, and the institution of slavery should remain untouched. When Lincoln removed McClellan from command after Antietam, the "young Napoleon" returned to private life. But he made no secret of his opposition to the administration's emancipation policy or his personal disdain for the president. By mid-1863 McClellan's Democratic friends were urging him to take a larger role in national politics.

These temporary political flurries should not obscure the remarkable legislative record of the 37th Congress or Lincoln's success in accomplishing most of his early goals. In fact these conflicts—or at least the form they took—may have been instrumental in smoothing the way to the Union's ultimate success. Compare the situation of the Confederacy. In the antebellum years most of the South had only one functioning party. Once the conflict was underway, dissenting opinion had no opportunity to coalesce around an opposition party. Consequently for much of the war Jefferson Davis was plagued by critics on all sides with no partisan tools at his disposal to control the situation. Lincoln's party included Republicans of various stripes, but extreme opinions were held in check by the bonds of party loyalty and the promise of political patronage. Moreover, the administration's most vigorous opponents were in the Democratic party, a recognized vehicle for dissent. In contrast, Davis's strongest opponents—in Richmond or in the Southern statehouses—were a formless mass, undifferentiated by party identification. In the absence of a two-party system the Confederate president had no established routes to reward his supporters or place sanctions on those dissenters within his own party.

The successes at Gettysburg and Vicksburg in the summer of 1863 were, in retrospect, instrumental in assuring an ultimate Union victory. Five months later Lincoln journeyed to Gettysburg to participate in the dedication of the Gettysburg National Cemetery. In his short address there he reminded the assembled audience of the history of their nation "conceived in liberty, and dedicated to the proposition that all men are created equal." He went on to stress "the unfinished work" ahead.

By the time the dead had been buried at Gettysburg the United States had made the military and political adjustments necessary to fight a long war. In so doing the nation's leadership had gone well beyond the haphazard structure that had stumbled into the First Battle of Bull Run. Their decisions had been felt throughout Northern society. Women and men on the home front had adjusted to conscription, greenbacks, emancipation, political arrests, and—most important—staggering casualty rates. The next question is, how did the people of the North react to these changes during two and a half tumultuous years?

4

Manpower Adjustments

IN THE SPRING of 1861 most Americans, both Union and Confederate, assumed that the Civil War would peak quickly and resolve itself just as fast, perhaps in a single glorious confrontation. The North's young men clamored for a piece of the excitement before it was too late. By summer this early naive spirit had given way to the realization that this would be more than a splendid little adventure. Over the next four years the Union's procedures for filling the ranks of its forces evolved from hastily arranged measures to a progressively sophisticated array of "carrots and sticks." In the process Northern communities witnessed the war's impact on traditional assumptions about localism, voluntarism, and individualism.

In the early days of the war a community could fill a military regiment by pitching a tent on the town green and hiring a band to play patriotic airs. The biggest challenge for the state governors, who were charged with administering the initial recruitment, was to find equipment for all the recruits while satisfying the scores of local leaders clamoring for military commissions. Before long, local and national leaders had to contemplate more active measures to attract men.

In the days after Fort Sumter the motivations for young men to enlist on both sides seemed wrapped up in the excitement of the moment: patriotic enthusiasm, the lure of adventure, an urge for vengeance. Even those Union soldiers who felt no sympathy for the slave often held a deep antagonism for the slaveholder. Many Southerners acted to defend their homes from invasion and their institutions from destruction. Northerners saw the Confederacy as a threat, but in a more subtle sense. While the rebellion did not physically endanger the homes of most Northern volunteers, it did threaten the nation. Even if the conflict was over national ideals, individual soldiers translated such abstractions into much more immediate terms. Thus men on both sides fought for the protection of their own local communities. To such concerns we must add the powerful pull of honor. Men went to war as part of their perceived roles as protectors of family and community. Those who neglected the dictates of manhood were likely to face reminders from friends and family members.

As persuasive as these motivations may have been, by late 1861 they had already attracted the most likely recruits. Meanwhile, furloughed troops returned home with tales of poor conditions, shoddy equipment, and incompetent officers. After a disastrous secession winter the wartime economy slowly began to heat up, providing enhanced employment opportunities at home. Even if the stream of willing enlistees never dried up completely, the government had to go beyond mere oratory to fill its armies as casualties mounted and the calls grew for more men. One answer to this rising manpower dilemma was to improve financial inducements to enlist. Willing recruits could be offered substantial bonuses upon enlistment. A further option was to turn to some form of military conscription. Yet another strategy was somehow to convince citizens on the home front that they should undertake more vigorous recruiting measures at the local level. The North's evolving wartime policies combined all these tactics.

At the onset of war the United States Army had just over 16,000 officers and men. Roughly a third of the nation's 313 officers gave up their commissions and joined the Confederacy. The Union had to start nearly from scratch in preparing for war. Both the Union and the Confederacy chose to organize their armies around state regiments rather than relying on federal troops. In response to the firing on Fort Sumter, Lincoln called for 75,000 ninety-day militiamen under an old statute that allowed him to call state militias into federal service. A few weeks later he asked for 42,000 three-year volunteers and more men to expand the navy and supplement federal forces. That July, the day after the First Battle of Bull Run, Lincoln took advantage of new congressional authorization and called for an additional half-million three-year men. In these and later calls the numbers were apportioned in quotas to each state. By the close of 1861 the Union Army numbered roughly 700,000 men, mostly three-year volunteers in state regiments. (Many of these men had been among the initial 90,000 three-month troops, who reenlisted when their terms expired.)

At full strength a Union regiment consisted of ten companies of one hundred men each. Regiments marched under state numerals—the 69th Pennsylvania Volunteers, the 6th Massachusetts—and individual companies were often recruited out of single neighborhoods or communities. The structure reinforced the local allegiances that underlay the national cause. Moreover, many companies and some regiments took on distinctly ethnic flavors. Many immigrant company rolls were filled with familiar Irish or German surnames. Others had a more exotic flavor. New York's Garibaldi Guards were predominantly Italian, including officers who had seen combat with the famed Italian nationalist, but it also included Hungarians, French, Spaniards, and Croats. In Chicago in April 1861 a Swedish army veteran formed a company of Swedes.

As the war wore on the process of reinforcement tended

to maintain these distinctive identities. Regiments home on leave recruited new members to replenish their depleted ranks. When young men came of age they hoped to join their older neighbors and siblings. But generally such efforts could not keep up with the Civil War's attrition. By mid-war regiments regularly marched into battle with only a fraction of their normal complement of troops. Unlike the practice in later wars, military authorities preferred to create new regiments of raw recruits rather than insert untried men among seasoned veterans. One result of these policies was that both new and veteran regiments tended to maintain a connection to the home front. Newspapers covered the military progress generally but reserved their most detailed scrutiny for the exploits of the local boys. Letters home reported on the activities of friends and relatives; correspondence to the camps was sometimes passed around from tent to tent. In such a world soldiers felt they were fighting as members of a community as well as part of a state regiment or a national army.

The system of recruiting and reinforcement contributed to the sense that this was a "citizens' war" waged by brothers fighting side by side. The command structure further emphasized both the war's democratic aspects and its fundamentally localistic nature. In most instances volunteers claimed the right to elect their own company-grade officers (lieutenants and captains). These men in turn selected the regiment's field-grade officers. This system may have served to elevate the community's most respected men into leadership positions, but in the field it initially had its drawbacks. Those elected officers who had earned the respect of their comrades in peacetime were not necesssarily born to military command. And even those with the requisite talent learned that a battlefield is no place for participatory democracy. At the other end of the command structure the Union also wrestled with the conflicting pulls of military necessity and political expediency. Governors dispensed military commissions to party favorites; Lincoln carefully balanced military commands along geographic, ethnic, and political lines.

The task of organizing Union recruiting was the responsibility of the War Department under the direction of Secretary Simon Cameron. Unfortunately the Pennsylvania politician proved an inept administrator whose department was hounded by charges of corruption. In late 1861 he resigned, and Lincoln replaced him with the crusty former Democrat Edwin M. Stanton. Although often a political annoyance, Stanton directed a generally efficient War Department through the next three and a half years.

Even before Stanton took office, the flow of willing recruits had slowed to a trickle. In April 1862 the new secretary of war temporarily suspended all recruiting activities in a measure which seemed to combine a mistaken assumption that the North already had enough men in uniform with a general concern about the Union's inefficient recruiting system. That July, in the wake of McClellan's failure outside Richmond, Lincoln recognized that the earlier optimism was misplaced and called for another 300,000 volunteers. The president hoped that vigorous efforts by the state governors would help meet the need, but in Washington the pressure for a draft was mounting.

Disheartened by the poor response to the latest call for troops, Congress enacted the Militia Act on July 17. The bill ordered the enrollment of men between ages eighteen and forty-five and gave the president power to conscript state militias into federal service for up to nine months. Under this law the governors retained power over the state drafts, but where the states lacked draft apparatus—which was often the case—the president was authorized to order "all necessary rules and regulations" to execute the bill. The following month the War Department announced a call for 300,000 nine-month militia, and Stanton began setting the framework for a draft in those states where there was no established system. Each county would have a draft commissioner and enrolling officer appointed by the governor. Men in certain occupations—including government officials, some civil servants, and war industry workers—were to be exempt, and those men selected would have the option of hiring a substitute. The August call-up, coming close on the heels of July's levy of 300,000 three-year men, triggered a hopelessly complex series of calculations and negotiations. The War Department assigned quotas to individual states based on population. Rather than insist on 600,000 men, Stanton agreed to count each three-year volunteer as the equivalent of four nine-month men. Thus 375,000 three-year men would have met the original bill. In fact this round of recruiting and conscription yielded nearly 90,000 nine-month men and more than 420,000 three-year volunteers, well in excess of the stated objectives. But these figures were not easily achieved.

Although most observers agreed that some sort of conscription measure had become necessary, in practice the first draft was cloaked in controversy from the outset. The complex quota system unleashed a great many complaints about unfair calculations. Even where the rules were properly followed, their intricacy left observers muttering about federal mismanagement and duplicity. Most states allowed draftees to furnish substitutes, leading to charges of class bias. And as long as local officials administered the draft, rumors flew of special favors and other irregularities. In one Connecticut town the local selectmen charged with assembling the enrollment list simply removed their own names before the drawing. In addition to routine claims of corruption, the draft suffered from inconsistent state policies, particularly concerning exemptions. New York, for instance, excluded college professors, teachers, and students; the same individuals would have been subject to conscription in neighboring Connecticut.

After much public discussion, most states successfully met

their assigned quotas without resorting to a militia draft. And where drafts were held they generally came off without incident. But in a few places—including Midwest Copperhead strongholds in Ohio and Indiana, and the eastern Pennsylvania coal fields—the enrolling officers met with violent resistance. Secretary Stanton remained dissatisfied with the awkward complexities inherent in this mixed state-federal system of conscription. Unless this latest round of recruits and conscripts could bring the war to a close, new legislation seemed likely.

Implementation of a state militia draft coincided with a mounting debate over the use of black troops. Although blacks had served in earlier American wars, and black sailors had long been a part of the United States Navy, many Northerners resisted the idea of black army volunteers. Abolitionists, both black and white, saw black military service as an important step toward enhancing black rights. More callous citizens embraced any plan that would preserve white lives. A provision of the July 1862 Militia Act authorized the president to enroll blacks for military service, but as long as the stated aim of the war was Union rather than emancipation, Lincoln resisted any such measure. But in August 1862 the Union began arming freedmen in South Carolina, and by the following year federal agents were busy recruiting black volunteers throughout the North. By the end of the war 179,000 black soldiers—mostly from the South—and 20,000 black sailors had served the Union cause.

The Union's military disappointments continued through the final months of 1862 into 1863. Meanwhile, recruiting continued to lag, and calls for further conscription mounted. In March 1863, after lengthy debate, the 37th Congress passed the Enrollment Act, taking responsibility for conscription out of the governors' hands. The federal draft, run by Provost Marshal General James B. Fry, eliminated some of the inefficiencies and local variations that plagued the

1862 militia draft. But the resulting process continued to rely on localized voluntary efforts for its success. Under the new law ablebodied men between twenty and forty-five were eligible for a federal draft (married men over thirty-five were placed in a secondary category), with federally appointed provost marshals in each congressional district charged with enrolling men in preparation for a call-up. When the administration determined that more troops were needed— as it would do four more times—Fry distributed quotas to the 185 enrollment districts long in advance of the draft day. Any community that filled its quota was spared the indignity and tension of a draft. When the draft day arrived, the local draft commission supervised a public drawing of sufficient names to assure that the required numbers of eligible men would be selected. The names of the drafted men were published, and the draft commissioners delivered notices requiring the draftees to appear for inspection.

Those men who found their names among the draftees must have felt a range of emotions from fear to humiliation to simple annoyance. Certainly the most willing participants would not have waited to see if their names would be drawn. But men hoping to avoid service still had several avenues available. One option was to claim one of the many available exemptions. Very few occupational exemptions survived, but allowances were made for men who could demonstrate one of fifty-one "diseases and infirmities"— ranging from club feet to excessive stammering—and hardship exemptions were granted for draftees with various family obligations. For men who could find no usuable exemption, the option remained to hire a substitute. Until 1864 draftees could avoid service by paying a $300 commutation fee. In many communities men who were liable for conscription pooled money—perhaps $100 each—in draft insurance clubs that would hire substitutes for those members who were selected. Some churches even assessed members of the congregation to purchase the release of drafted members.

Most men who claimed that military service violated their religious scruples were content to pay the commutation fee to avoid service. But some Quakers balked at financially supporting the war effort and resisted friends' efforts to pay the fee for them. A few attracted widespread attention by refusing to obey orders or in any way cooperate with their military superiors. Upon hearing of the plight of Vermont Quaker Cyrus Pringle, President Lincoln interceded on his behalf. In December 1863 the provost marshal general paroled all conscripted Quakers and ordered that none others be forced into uniform until they were "called for." (This decision merely ratified what had become common practice in some localities.)

More important for understanding how the draft really worked were the community strategies aimed at avoiding the draft altogether. Only those districts that failed to fill their assigned quotas had to face a draft. By leaving fifty days from the announcement of a call-up to the actual draft day, Fry gave each district ample time to recruit men by other means. Often even the threat of a draft had little initial effect. But as the day approached, newspaper headlines grew larger and more urgent, spurring on local citizens to greater efforts. When the appointed day arrived, many districts had met their quotas or faced only negligible drafts.

How were recruits found? From early on in the war the North learned to rely on progressively higher bounties to fill its ranks. Within a month after Fort Sumter new three-year recruits received $100 bounties upon enlistment. In late 1863 the federal government raised the bounty to $300 for new recruits and $400 for reenlistees. Soon a multitiered system emerged in which state and local governments grafted their own bounties onto the established federal offering. Citizens who were anxious to save their communities from the draft contributed to vigorous bounty fund drives. Whereas in mid-1861 recruiting posters had called for "A Few Select Men," now passionate patriots were told to give money to help "Avoid the Draft." In some cities adjoining wards entered bidding wars for available recruits. In the war's first few years Deerfield, Massachusetts, turned to local "sons" to fill recruiting quotas; by mid-war the New England community was relying on paid recruits from less wealthy neighboring towns. By the close of the war volunteers in some areas earned more than $1,000 for signing up.

The bounty system, spurred on by the threat of conscription, succeeded in enticing new men into service, but not without costs. Like the conscripts, men who enlisted solely for the bounty were not always ideal soldiers. Many "jumped" from service at the first opportunity, sometimes to reenlist under a new name for another large bounty. Moreover, the bounty system spawned a class of unsavory bounty agents who proved adept at separating naive recruits from their newfound wealth.

Some communities acted even more aggressively to spare their citizens from service. After several days of bloody draft riots in July 1863, New York City established a fund, financed through the sale of bonds, to pay the commutation costs of poor draftees who were unable to furnish a substitute. Chicago's aldermen instituted a war tax to provide stipends for the families of soldiers, pay bounties to new recruits, and, if necessary, hire substitutes for local conscripts. Towns and cities across the North followed suit, using bond sales, taxation, and voluntary funds to offer bounties, pay commutation fees, and hire substitutes.

Despite all the attention accompanying the North's March 1863 Enrollment Act, relatively few federal draftees actually served in the Union Army. The four national call-ups yielded roughly 46,000 conscripts while another 118,000 men who were "held to service" hired substitutes. Taken together, conscripts (3.7 percent) and substitutes (9.35 percent) accounted for only about 13 percent of the 1,260,000 new troops raised after the federal draft took effect. The Confederate draft, in contrast, produced more than 20 percent of the Southern army. Pre-1863 data are much weaker, but it appears that the state militia drafts generated roughly 87,500 nine-month conscripts, or just over 11 percent of the troops raised in the war's first two years. Overall, only about 5.5 percent of the men who fought for the Union served as conscripts, and most of these were nine-month men.

If Congress passed the Enrollment Act to fill the Union Army with conscripts, the bill does not seem to have functioned well. But as a measure to spur citizens to more vigorous recruiting, it seems much better. By late 1862 Northern recruiters had begun to discover that neither patriotic appeals nor the financial "carrot" of bonuses would indefinitely fill the ranks. The various waves of conscription added a new "stick" to the equation. But the threat of conscription was not really directed at young men so much as it was at individual towns and urban wards. Thus the message to communities was plain: "Find some way to fill your quotas or you will face a draft." Localities responded with renewed recruiting enthusiasm: voluntary groups raised bounty funds; aldermen passed taxes and floated bonds; threatening headlines grew larger as the appointed day approached. As the federal conscription system matured, regulations encouraged this process. The provost marshal general announced local quotas and scheduled draft days long in advance, providing ample opportunity for the recruiting frenzy to build. In short, the Union's conscription legislation worked by giving the North's traditional localism an extra shove.

How representative was the Union Army of the total population? Was it a cross section of the Northern population, or did specific groups bear a disproportionate burden?

Available data defy exact calculations, but roughly 35 percent of the North's white men who were between thirteen and forty-three in 1860 served in the Union Army or Navy (the Confederate figure was about 61 percent). Like all wars, the Civil War was fought primarily by young men. The median age of Union troops at enlistment was about 23.5 years; nearly two-fifths enlisted before their twenty-first birthday. One scholar has estimated that at mid-war three-fourths of the Union Army was still under the age of thirty. One study of two New Hampshire towns found married men less likely to enlist than unmarried men, but much of that difference disappeared when the author excluded eighteen- and nineteen-year-olds (who were largely unmarried and enlisted in great numbers). Certainly many volunteers left behind wives and children, but most were probably still unmarried.

One of the great clichés about the Civil War is that the North filled its army with recently arrived immigrants. Many immigrants did prove their patriotism by serving in the Union ranks. And in the war's final years, some Northern towns turned to foreign-born men to help fill their draft quotas. Still, only about a quarter of the Northern army was composed of immigrants, as compared with 30 percent of the military-age population. Why this underrepresentation? First, although generous bounties and high substitute fees certainly attracted many immigrant men, the Enrollment Act exempted aliens from conscription. And second, Irish and German Catholic immigrants generally rejected Republican policies—especially emancipation—and thus may have been less inclined to enlist in the Union cause.

Critics of the Union's recruitment efforts charged that the provisions for bounties, substitutes, and commutation fees turned the conflict into a "rich man's war and a poor man's fight." Was this a fair criticism? It depends on how we phrase the question. Certainly the Enrollment Act enabled wealthy men to avoid service with ease. *Fincher's Trades' Review*, a leading labor newspaper, declared that "this allowing a citizen to shirk his duty simply because he has means at his command is anti–Republican and should be discarded." Rather, young men of all classes should be required to serve, "and should stern fate bring a millionaire's son cheek by jowl with a sturdy mechanic, ere the campaigns are over, perhaps both may be benefitted by the contact."

But while contemporaries pointed to obvious inequities in the conscription system, the Union Army was surprisingly representative of the Northern population. A comparison of the previous occupations of more than 660,000 Union troops with the occupational distribution among Northern men in the 1860 census seems to contradict the familiar charge. Farmers and farm laborers made up the largest occupational category in both the military sample (47.5 percent) and in the antebellum census (42.9 percent). Roughly a quarter of the antebellum men (24.9 percent) were listed as skilled laborers and another 16.7 percent were semiskilled; the sampled soldiers reported nearly identical figures (25.1 percent and 15.9 percent). The only clear disparity appears to have been at the upper occupational ranks. Only one soldier in twenty described himself as a white-collar or commercial worker; 10 percent of the men in the 1860 census fit that description. But this is hardly surprising when we remember that nearly all Union soldiers were fairly young men, whereas the census included older men who had had much longer to rise into the ranks of the professional classes.

Leaving aside the aggregate data, how did conscription affect individual Northern men? Most of the white men who had not enlisted and were subject to the draft in mid-1863 probably preferred not to serve. How might such a man stay out of uniform? One strategy was to stay off the enrollment officer's list altogether. In some Copperhead neighborhoods, locals refused to cooperate in identifying eligible men, and occasionally enrollment officers reported meeting violent resistance. Unwilling soldiers could also provide inaccurate information. In one Philadelphia precinct in 1862 seventeen men said they were forty-four years old and thus eligible for the draft, whereas an astonishing forty-three reported that they were forty-six years of age—a year over the limit. Other men simply slipped through the cracks by giving false names or addresses. Men who disdained such unscrupulous routes could improve their chances of avoiding service by joining in the recruiting frenzy as draft day approached. In this sense the personal and communal intermingled. Donations to bounty fund drives answered the patriotic call to fill local quotas while lessening the chance that one's own name—or that of a loved one— would appear on the eventual list of draftees.

Even if selected, draftees still had numerous options for avoiding service. Provost Marshal General Fry's final report indicates that nearly 777,000 names were drawn in the four federal drafts between 1863 and 1865. These men were expected to appear for inspection on an appointed day. But the draft boards examined only about two-thirds (522,000) of those selected. More than 160,000 (21 percent) draftees "failed to report" to the boards and another 93,000 (12 percent) were discharged without examination, generally because the quota had already been filled. Of those who did report, medical examiners excused 160,000 (31 percent) for physical or mental disabilities; 155,000 (30 percent) received exemption because of age, alien status, family hardship, or the like. Thus only 206,678 men (26.6 percent of the total drawn and 39.5 percent of those inspected) were officially "held to service" in the four call-ups.

Those men who were "held to service" either had to pay the commutation fee, produce a substitute, or enter service as a conscript. In the first two federal drafts, most conscripts chose to pay the $300 commutation fee. When new legislation restricted that option, many more turned to the substitute market. Overall 86,724 draftees (42 percent) paid the commutation fee and 73,607 (35 percent) hired substitutes. Thus the 777,000 initial names yielded only 46,347 conscripts, or roughly 1 percent of the Northern white men of military age.

Clearly the trip from enrollment to selection to formal conscription was a long one with numerous opportunities to avoid military service. What is known about the men who chose each route? The 160,000 who "failed to report" are in many senses the most intriguing and elusive group. One historian has studied those congressional districts with the highest proportion of "skedaddlers" and offered a few tentative conclusions. Illegal draft evasion increased steadily over the course of the war. In the first two federal call-ups illegal draft evasion was concentrated in Wisconsin, Michigan, New York, and Pennsylvania, largely in districts with heavy immigrant Catholic, non-Republican populations. In the final two drafts illegal evasion spread geographically and demographic correlations weakened. This shift may have reflected a broadening dissatisfaction with the war as well as a response to the removal of the commutation clause, which drove up substitute prices.

Evidence from the Thirtieth District of New York provides a small glimpse into the occupations of those men who failed to report following the war's final draft. In this Democratic district in Erie County, 44 percent of the illegal evaders and only 22 percent of the men who furnished substitutes were unskilled workers. Conversely, white-collar and commercial workers made up 28 percent of the men who hired substitutes and only 12 percent of the skedaddlers. This suggests that although some men of all classes failed to report, draftees with greater means were better prepared to use the legal means of draft avoidance. But this may not be the whole story. More than two-thirds of the Thirtieth District's illegal evaders were foreign-born, supporting the argument that immigrants particularly resisted the draft.

The occupational data on those men who reported for inspection reveals more about the role of class in avoiding service. One sample of nearly five thousand men who received medical exemptions exhibited an occupational distribution very similar to that of all white men in the 1860 census, except that white-collar and commercial workers were slightly overrepresented. In a parallel study of one thousand men exempted as aliens, 35 percent were listed as unskilled workers as opposed to 17 percent nationwide. These exemptions, then, cut in opposite directions. Aliens were more likely to come from the lower occupational categories, whereas white-collar workers may have been more successful in pleading their cases to medical examiners.

What of those men who were actually "held to service"? Once again the occupational data are incomplete, but one study of more than fourteen thousand men reveals some rather strong patterns. Three-fourths of the men sampled paid commutation fees or hired substitutes; the remaining 25 percent were conscripted. Nearly 95 percent of the sampled white-collar and commercial draftees purchased their freedom as did 88 percent of the professionals. In contrast only 65 percent of the unskilled laborers and 69 percent of the farmers and farm workers were able to avoid conscription through this route.

Although the Union Army was not a perfect cross section of Northern society, it was much more representative than one might assume from reading the provisions of the Enrollment Act. Most soldiers fought because they wanted to; most who wished to avoid service probably succeeded. This is not to deny the economic biases inherent in the system. A wealthy man could purchase a substitute without discomfort, congratulating himself that he had done his patriotic duty. A poor man from an economically drained community might have been forced to choose between forced service or illegal evasion.

Northern efforts to fill the ranks—like much of the home-front experience—revealed an intricate tangle of traditional, localized efforts and newly centralized federal measures. The 1863 Enrollment Act was national legislation administered by federal officials; but its success depended on the energetic actions of thousands of local officials and private citizens.

The recruiting chronology is also indicative of the Civil War's larger patterns. In the first months passionate enthusiasm seemed to suffice. As the demand for men grew, policymakers experimented with various conscription acts while local citizens developed increasingly sophisticated means to organize recruiting. With time the balance between local and federal authority shifted, and the power vested in statehouses and governors' mansions declined. Despite these changes the essential keys to the North's recruiting success remained quite familiar: volunteers clustered in traditional associational webs; communities acted locally to fill their own quotas; and market forces—not legislation—dictated bounty levels and substitute costs.

How does this compare with the Confederacy's experience? Here too the story mirrors the war's central themes. First, the two sides were fundamentally similar in their responses to the Civil War's challenges. After first relying upon volunteers, during the war's second year the Confederate legislature turned to a conscription system that shared much in common with its Northern adversary, including provisions for exemptions, substitutes, and bounties for enlistees.

The differences between the two nations suggest a second recurring theme: the Confederacy had to make do with fewer men and inferior resources. In order to survive for four years the rebels had to put an extraordinarily high share of their eligible men into uniform. Thus the South turned to the draft earlier than the North and relied more heavily on conscripts to fight the war. With the Confederate economy in shambles, bounties never added up to much, and substitute prices became exorbitant before the government ended them altogether in late 1863. Early in the war Southerners were granted exemptions for various occupations, and—in a highly controversial provision—plantations with twenty or more slaves could declare one white man exempt from the draft. But later legislation closed such loopholes while widening the draft net to include men between seventeen and fifty. This evolving legislation—contrasted to the North—is bleak testimony to the Confederacy's numerical and financial limitations.

5

Emotional and Intellectual Adjustments

APPRAISING THE WAR'S "emotional and intellectual" effects combines deeply individual questions with broader matters of community and culture. How did citizens respond to the war's death and destruction? What was the effect of separation on those left behind? How did the ebb and flow on the battlefield change the civic culture at home? In fact, Northerners' responses to the war combined aspects of their familiar peacetime existence with various adaptations to the realities of the conflict. Distinctions between public and private frequently blurred. Thus a regiment's departure for the front was an occasion for hundreds of small personal dramas as well as a setting for a carefully choreographed civic ritual.

The Civil War was the nation's bloodiest conflict. Its roughly 620,000 military casualties are nearly equal to America's combined losses in every other war before Vietnam. The figures are even more sobering when considered in the light of the total population at the time. More than 180 of every 100,000 Americans suffered military deaths during the Civil War, a rate that was *six times* as high as that for World War II. Only the American Revolution, which took the lives of

118 out of every 100,000 Americans, approached the Civil War death toll.

The Civil War casualty rates are unique because Americans died on both sides. Roughly 8 percent of all white men of military age (between thirteen and forty-three in 1860) fell during the war. For the Northern states this figure was slightly lower at 6 percent; the Confederacy lost young men at three times that rate. This gap closes somewhat if we concentrate on those white men who served in uniform: a quarter of all Confederate soldiers died during the war as compared with one in six white Union troops. The North's black troops were less likely to fall in battle but twice as likely to die of disease, a disparity which reflects inequity in both assignments and medical treatment.

Mid-nineteenth-century Americans had a familiarity with death and dying that may seem strange to a modern reader. Loved ones generally spent their final days at home, surrounded by family and friends, rather than in hospitals or nursing homes. In this world the rituals of death took on great significance. Survivors found comfort in hearing and recording the deceased's final words, perhaps cutting a lock of hair as a final remembrance. In one of the most memorable moments in Harriet Beecher Stowe's *Uncle Tom's Cabin*, Little Eva gathers her family and friends around her death bed as she hands each one of her curls. This melancholy scene became one of the most famous tableaux of the antebellum decade.

During the first months of the Civil War Northerners applied their personal understanding of death to the Union's fallen heroes. In May 1861 Colonel Elmer Ellsworth, a flamboyant member of the New York Zouaves and a personal favorite of Abraham Lincoln, was killed while removing a Confederate flag flying in Alexandria, Virginia. As one of the war's first martyrs, Ellsworth became the focus of widespread public mourning. Soon death became commonplace, and only the loss of a major military leader attracted such national attention. But the passage of time did not harden hearts to those deaths that struck close to home. As the death tolls mounted one New York woman wrote, "We ought to remember that for every one that falls on the battlefield or suffers a languishing death in the hospitals, some friends mourn and weep their lives away." Northerners filled their diaries and letters with fears that their own loved ones might fall. The safe return of one young man prompted Rebecca Gratz to write: "He is a brave soldier—but I am a very coward for those I love." We can only imagine how Corporal J. L. Smith's mother reacted to these words from her son: "I write very long letters as we are being killed so fast. This may be my last."

Time and again home-front survivors struggled to place battlefield deaths into their familiar world of mourning, even though most bodies were buried hundreds of miles from home, often in unmarked graves. Family members took comfort when comrades wrote detailed letters describing their loved ones' final minutes. In one particularly tragic episode, a young lieutenant was shot in the head when he rushed to a dying general's side to hear his last words. Over the course of several months hospital volunteer Susan Trautwine grew particularly attached to one sixteen-year-old soldier. After the boy died she "combed back his hair from his cold forehead, kissed it twice for his mother & sister & cut his soft hair for them, keeping a small lock for myself." She also wrote to his sister, "telling her all I knew about him" and adding, "I feel almost certain that he has gone to God." In this fashion Northerners helped each other cope with missed deathbed scenes.

As individuals strove to cope with personal loss and communities grappled with shared grief, Americans tried to make some larger sense of the war's enormous costs. According to the historian Gerald Linderman, the first Civil War volunteers marched off to war with a clear "constellation of values," with courage as the centerpiece. But the lesson of the battlefield was that abstractions such as manliness, godliness, and honor provided little protection in this war. Linderman argues that as these war-weary veterans became disillusioned by their own experience, they grew frustrated with noncombatants at home who clung to the old beliefs. Certainly it was easier to romanticize death from the comfort of home. Although twice as many men died of disease as of wounds, newspapers avoided hospital reports in favor of accounts of battlefield deaths. On the other hand, this was the first war that civilians could view through the camera's eye. Battlefield photographs, such as Alexander Gardner's grim studies of corpses at Antietam, brought the war's true price home with awful realism.

At the same time the war's rising costs led some Northerners to cling more enthusiastically to the values that had led them to war. Ralph Waldo Emerson consoled the parents of a fallen soldier by suggesting that "one whole generation might well consent to perish, if, by their fall, political liberty & clean & just life could be made sure to the generations that follow." Or, as Abraham Lincoln reminded his audience at Gettysburg in November 1863: "It is rather for us to be here dedicated to the great task remaining before us—that from these honored dead we take increased devotion to that cause for which they gave the last full measure of devotion—that we here highly resolve that these dead shall not have died in vain...." Other Northerners explained the losses by portraying their cause as a holy war for abolition. And some saw a connection between the rule of God and the rule of law, with the rebels as the enemies of both.

While death and the fear of death cut deepest into the hearts of the women and men left behind, the personal pain of war began for hundreds of thousands of home-front Americans as soon as their loved ones marched off to battle. In his travels through the North in early 1862 Edward Dicey met a woman who claimed that "till within a year before, she could not recall the name of a single person whom she had ever known in the army, and...now she had sixty friends and relatives who were serving in the war." Like wartime deaths, these separations forced Northerners to forge new coping strategies from their familiar experiences.

The departure of volunteers for the front generally combined public ceremony with private leave-taking. By the time the first three-year regiments were leaving home in the summer of 1861, Northern communities had already begun to develop rituals to honor their volunteers. Great crowds lined the streets to watch the local boys pass by; martial music filled the air; and a military escort led the way. At the train station a local dignitary delivered a spirited address, and a group of patriotic women presented the troops with a hand-sewn battle flag. Local newspapers recorded each movement with loving detail. This pattern repeated itself time and again throughout the North. Sometimes the celebrations took on an ethnic flavor, reflecting the regiment's composition. On other occasions volunteer fire companies joined the parade honoring their departing brothers. With time some of the initial novelty wore off and the crowds diminished, but each departure still drew a host of well-wishers.

The community's connection to the local troops continued long after their trains had departed for the front. Men and women on the home front followed the Union's progress with the aid of extensive reporting in the Northern newspapers. In the antebellum years most Americans had rarely contemplated the world beyond their own community; now Civil War newspapers and magazines brought careful descriptions of far-off campaigns into homes throughout the North. Enthusiastic readers became amateur experts in military affairs, and at dinner tables and on streetcorners they second-guessed promotions and troop movements. Children accumulated specially printed photographs of their favorite generals as later generations would collect baseball cards.

This flood of information was aided by the changing state of technology. Battlefield reporters telegraphed stories home with previously unheard-of speed. When rumors of important clashes drifted northward, everyone from common citizens to Abraham Lincoln converged on the local telegraph office for the latest news. More than three thousand photographers pioneered their craft, bringing the war's visual images home to parlors and drawing rooms. Most papers rallied around the flag, although a few—like Horace Greeley's *New York Daily Tribune*—criticized Lincoln as too moderate. Some newspapers that were openly pro-secession in early 1861 were silenced by threatening patriotic mobs; others yielded to government censure. By mid-war the Democratic press had emerged as openly critical of administration policies, but most papers continued to support the war.

Civilians on the home front were most concerned with the exploits of the local troops. As Reid Mitchell has pointed out, the battle flags presented at their departure came to symbolize the volunteers' links with home. When they defended the flag they were not simply fighting for "Union" or "nation," they were defending their families and communities. Newspapers paid particular attention to the movements of local regiments, taking care to list the names of their own fallen heroes.

The most detailed information came from the soldiers themselves. By the fall of 1861 mail traveled to and from the camps at an extraordinary rate. People at home came to depend on regular correspondence to learn of their loved ones' safety and good health. Young wives grew restive if they did not hear from their husbands for even two weeks. Letters home commonly reported on the activities of relatives, friends, and neighbors in the same regiment. All this communication between soldiers and the home front meant that Northern communities continued to play a role in the lives of their sons at war. "Honor" and "duty" took on a different meaning when the volunteers knew that their actions might become the subject of a comrade's letter home. And a man tempted by the various vices of camp life might think twice knowing that news of his behavior could find its way back to his wife or mother.

While communities celebrated local regiments and mourned their dead, such activities were easily incorporated into the normal routines of civic life. The far greater strain of separation occurred in the home, where families had to cope with the absence of sons, brothers, and husbands. Here too letters, furloughs, and visits to camps helped those at home maintain relationships with the volunteers. The historian is consistently struck by the ways in which civilians strove to maintain their traditional roles when corresponding with soldiers. Parents—and mothers in particular—filled their letters with warnings about the moral dangers of military life. One Oswego, New York, woman wrote to her son, "We was very glad to hear that swearing was prohibited in your company and hope that card playing and all such vices are also." Mothers also revealed an intense, if ill-informed, concern for their son's health and safety. On various occasions Hannah Smith asked her son if he ever sat on the ground, if his military "house" had windows, and if he would like her to send him a cat. Corporal Smith advised against the latter, warning that "the soldiers would mistake him for a rabbit."

Soldiers asked for all sorts of things. In early 1865 Michigan cavalryman Webster Teachout wrote to his mother, "I wish you would bake up about a dozen mince pies and two or three loaves of bread and some frid cakes and a saucage or so." The same soldier might request very different things from different family members, suggesting the continuation of antebellum roles. Seventeen-year-old William Thomas Jones received warm underwear from his mother; his sister sewed him a pair of gloves; and he asked his father to mail him a revolver. In a particularly revealing letter Jones asked brother Harry to "send me down a bottle of Chestnut Grove Whiskey for medicinal purposes"; and, he added, "Don't let the folks know it."

When their husbands decided to enlist, even the strongest women patriots struggled with their emotions. As Philadelphian Katherine Brinley Wharton prepared for her husband's departure, she asked herself, "What am I more than others that I should say I cannot give him up [?]" Once apart, some women begged their spouses to secure furloughs, whatever the cost. Iowan Jennie Thompson worried that her husband would grow too fond of military life: "You are liking the place so well and seem to enjoy a soldier's life so much I do not but think there is some danger of your liking it so well you will not care anything about living with me any more." In early 1863 Pennsylvanian Richard Ashhurst wrote home emphasizing "the importance of wives writing cheerful letters." Two officers in his regiment, he explained, had recently resigned their commissions after "receiving the most melancholy desponding letters from their wives."

During the Civil War women and men who rarely had occasion to write letters found themselves relying on the written word to reveal their deepest longings. Jennie Thompson wrote to her husband in the 20th Iowa Volunteers: "Oh, how I wish I could sleep with you tonight. Would you like to sleep with me? But I can only dream of being with you and that is very pleasant for I see you every night in my dreams." When John Lynch spent Christmas without his fiancée he had to turn to his own thoughts for comfort: "My darling how my thoughts have been following you all day. I have pictured you in all kind[s] of positions until my imagination has been tired out." One young woman wrote to her lover: "*I feel so bad to night. I think my heart will break. I worry so much about you. I cannot sleep sound no* more. I awaken up at night and lay for hours wondering if I ever shall see my dear Pet again."

Fears were greatest when word came that a loved one had been wounded in battle. When Julia Wheelock heard that her brother had been shot at the Battle of Chantilly, she visited fifteen hospitals across the South before learning that he had died. Sarah Chapin of Michigan read in a local newspaper that her husband had been wounded at the Battle of Murfreesboro. A month later, when she still had not learned his fate, Sarah wrote, "It seems to me sometimes as though i cannot possibly wait much longer without knowing...." Soon news arrived that Theodore Chapin was alive, but dying, in a Nashville hospital. Sarah ached to be by her husband's side but had to be content with regular letters back and forth.

Beyond these deep emotional strains, how did their husbands' departures change the everyday routines of Northern wives? Some studies of Southern women indicate major changes in their roles, as huge numbers of men joined the Confederate armies. According to this view, Southern women took on new responsibilities when men were unavailable to run farms, control slaves, and generally make economic decisions. In some instances impoverished Southern women entered the unfamiliar public arena by petitioning the Confederacy for material assistance. Other historians have emphasized strong continuity in the position of Southern women, insisting that the South remained grounded in patriarchal assumptions.

Northern women turned to extended networks of family and friends to help fill the void left by a husband's absence. Female diarists regularly reported special visits to the wives of military volunteers. Such communal adjustments were easier in the North than in the South, where a much greater percentage of white men were in uniform.

Although Northern families did not face the shortages that plagued the South, wives of soldiers suffered economic deprivation if they had to rely on their husbands' modest military wages. (This was particularly the case for the wives of black volunteers, who were paid less at every rank.) Some cities sought to encourage volunteering by establishing funds for the relief of families of volunteers.

Sometimes a husband tried to exercise paternal control even in his absence. When William G. Thompson left for war he insisted that his wife Jennie live with his family in Pennsylvania rather than remain home in Iowa among strangers. Theodore Chapin wrote to his wife from his Nashville deathbed with detailed instructions about how to deal with the family's debts upon his death. Other men regularly wrote home with directions on financial matters. Still, the evidence suggests that many women—on both sides of the Mason-Dixon line—experienced, and perhaps enjoyed, enhanced autonomy as they ran households in their husbands' absence.

Especially poignant situations arose when the Civil War split families. Sometimes these wrenchings involved couples from different parts of the country. Connecticut native Katherine Hubbell married a Georgian in 1860. When the war broke out her brother enlisted with the Union while her husband and his four brothers fought for the Confederacy. Southerner Septima Collis married a Northern soldier before the war, and her brother died in a Confederate uniform. In other instances the war's issues themselves divided families. Young diarist Sarah Butler Wister and her mother, famed actress Fanny Kemble, sided with the Union while her father, Pierce Butler, was an outspoken Southern sympathizer who was temporarily jailed for suspected treason. Abolitionist Republican Annie Cox spoke for many couples when she tried to protect her courtship with her Copperhead beau by telling him, "You and I shall have to agree to disagree."

While individuals faced difficult personal adjustments to wartime separation and death, much of Northern society carried on seemingly untouched by the conflict. After a few initial months of excited confusion, the North's cultural life nearly returned to normal. In late 1861 Boston music critic John Sullivan Dwight returned from several months in Europe to discover that "It is hard to realize that we are in the midst of civil war."

Even as local newspapers described bloody battlefield scenes, their entertainment sections reported large crowds attending cultural events ranging from the highbrow to the decidedly lowbrow. In the winter after Gettysburg, several major international opera companies toured the North to enthusiastic crowds. The *New York Musical World and Review* noted that despite early fears, "the amount of music heard in these years of trial...has certainly not diminished." The combined forces of economic prosperity and patriotic enthusiasm—assisted by the tariff on imported sheet music— triggered a boom in popular music publishing. The theater too prospered through the nation's crisis. Actors Edwin Forrest and Edwin Booth continued to perform for large crowds. Some houses responded to the national crisis by including one-act plays with patriotic themes as part of an evening's entertainment. Advertisements promised customers spirited music and Union displays in addition to more traditional shows. In the meantime, a host of other popular spectacles suggested a nation hungry for diversions. P. T. Barnum continued to entertain huge audiences at his New York City museum; an immense crowd turned out to see the famed dwarf, General Tom Thumb, marry Miss Lavinia Warren. Each summer Northeasterners flocked to popular resorts from Niagara Falls to Cape May. Rural communities enjoyed regular visits from traveling circuses bringing with them a host of animal and human oddities. Gala picnics dotted the calendar in cities and towns.

Organized sports continued to expand as they had in peacetime. The new sport of baseball flourished on the home front while soldiers in military camps helped establish it as the national pastime. Only ten days after the Battle of Chancellorsville, the city of Charleston, Maryland—conveniently located on the railroad line between Philadelphia and Baltimore—hosted an enormous crowd for a sixty-one-round bareknuckle prizefight. The Union's horse racing enthusiasts saw the opening of several new Northern tracks because border-state breeders could no longer take their horses south. Even as anxious citizens pored over accounts from the battlefield, gamblers routinely gathered to bet on a wide assortment of cruel bloodsports, including cockfighting and "ratting" (involving dogs thrown into a pit of rats).

To some, such emphasis on entertainment smacked of frivolity in a time of national crisis. Critics complained when urban socialites staged massive balls while soldiers lay dying in hospitals and on battlefields. John Sullivan Dwight struggled with this contrast but concluded that although "the times of course demand sterner work...whatever rough necessities of war are forced upon us peaceful and peace-loving people, we cannot forget that peaceful things are all the while the real end of life, and we must carry on a steeled *life* of some sort, in times of war as well as of peace." In his study of Springfield, Massachusetts, the historian Michael Frisch found "an often frantic rhythm in the city's [wartime] social life" that seemed to turn the city into a "perpetual carnival" of parades, lectures, concerts, snake charmers, and even public demonstrations of laughing gas. But while others have attributed this gala atmosphere to Springfield's great wartime prosperity and general insulation from the war, Frisch offered the intriguing interpretation that the city's seemingly insatiable appetite for diversion was really a reaction to the Civil War's "underlying tensions."

For men and women of letters the Civil War offered its own set of challenges. The sectional conflict found Northern intellectuals divided over the nation's larger future. Some stressed the importance of individualism while warning of the dangers of excessive power. More conservative thinkers celebrated the collective power of institutions and welcomed any chance to impose authority and discipline on a society gone adrift. Most Northern intellectuals of all stripes disliked slavery, but they varied widely in the depth of their feeling.

The historian George Fredrickson has argued that the outbreak of the Civil War had the ironic effect of bringing intellectuals of wildly different views together in a common cause. Some saw it as an important step toward abolition, especially after Lincoln issued his Emancipation Proclamation. Walt Whitman worried less about slavery, instead viewing the war as a test of national manhood and essential to America's larger democratic mission. Ralph Waldo Emerson watched the outbreak of war with skepticism. But he soon embraced the Union cause with the zeal of a convert, calling on the nation to cleanse itself of rebel impurities. Emerson even waded into the whirl of partisan politics, characterizing the Republicans as the "Party of Hope," at odds with the Democratic "Party of Memory." Conservatives emphasized the war as an ideal route to national moral regeneration. As George Templeton Strong saw it, "Without the shedding of blood there is no remission of sins." Despite this shared patriotism, Fredrickson saw an important wartime tension between antiinstitutional humanitarians (the strongest individualists) and those who hoped that the war would accelerate the triumph of centralization, efficiency, and nationalism.

Some Northern writers chronicled their personal experiences as home-front volunteers. In December 1862 Louisa May Alcott began work at a Washington hospital ministering to soldiers wounded at Fredericksburg. Within a month, illness drove Alcott out of the hospital, and she returned home to write her *Hospital Sketches*. Walt Whitman, too old for soldiering at forty-three, threw himself into hospital work with tremendous energy. Although he never witnessed a battle, for three years the author of *Leaves of Grass* visited young men in Washington's military hospitals. In *Drum Taps*, a widely circulated collection of wartime poems, Whitman sought to capture the mood of the hospital, but too often he stopped short of portraying the war's true carnage. Even in his letters home to his mother, Whitman muted his portrait of the horrors of war by portraying a martial spirit that continued to entice him. In the week before Gettysburg, Whitman's blood surged as he watched a military parade passing through town: "I tell you it had the look of *real war*—noble looking fellows; a man feels so proud on a good horse, and armed." But a few sentences later he added: "Alas! how many of these healthy, handsome, rollicking young men will lie cold in death before the apples ripen in the orchard[?]"

In his study of Civil War–era writers Daniel Aaron concluded that although the war certainly touched most authors, many avoided full immersion in the conflict. Henry Adams watched the war from the safety of London; William Dean Howells served as U.S. consul in Venice; Henry James, Jr., remained in New England. Mark Twain initially cast his lot with the Rebel Home Guards in Missouri, but soon he went to join his brother in Nevada, far away from the excitement and horror of war. Yet even Emily Dickinson, who studiously avoided almost all news of the outside world, found the trauma of war filtering into her poetry. Others, Aaron argues, neither rallied to the cause nor celebrated the redeeming value of war. Nathaniel Hawthorne disliked slavery and generally agreed that the South should be punished for secession, but he never shared the patriotic enthusiasms of his countrymen. Instead Hawthorne remained pessimistic and detached as the two sides pounded away at each other. "We seem," he wrote "to have little, or at least a very misty idea of what we are fighting for." Ardent nationalist Herman Melville had little animosity toward the South and serious doubts about the abolitionists. While other authors celebrated heroism and noble causes, Melville presented in his *Battle Pieces* what Aaron called "a parable of human blindness."

Although many of America's leading thinkers struggled with the war's larger meaning, no writer fully captured the war's magnitude. Military veterans produced some of the most noteworthy works of the conflict. John William De-Forest's *Miss Ravenel's Conversion from Secession to Loyalty* included a realism that reflected the author's battlefield experience. Union veteran Ambrose Bierce's harrowing and often surreal stories of battle offer no room for heroic ideas or sentimentalism.

At the other end of the literary spectrum the war certainly generated a boom in more popular publications. Bookstores hawked military biographies, infantry manuals, hastily published memoirs, and all manner of war-related works. Sentimental fiction for readers of all ages poured from Northern presses. New Yorker Henry Morford's three home-front novels—*The Days of Shoddy, Shoulder Straps,* and *The Coward*—followed a romantic formula while assailing Northerners for war profiteering, military incompetence, and other sins.

Despite the war's failure to spawn great literature, the intellectual life of the North remained active. Public lectures continued to be a popular diversion, and libraries reported expanded activity. The experiences of colleges reflect the war's varied effects. In the fervor after Fort Sumter, college students threw themselves into military drilling, often forming their own companies. Yale, Harvard, and Princeton all reported diminished numbers, with a third of the Princetonians returning home to the Confederacy. Nonetheless, colleges prospered and expanded, reflecting the wartime prosperity. At least fourteen new schools opened their doors in the midst of the conflict. And in July 1862 Congress passed the Morrill Act, granting public lands to each state for the establishment of agricultural and mechanical colleges.

The mixed impact of the war is shown most strikingly in

religion, which had played an increasingly central role in the lives of most antebellum Northerners. In the first enthusiasm for war, organized religion appeared to withdraw, as all eyes turned to the military camps and battlefields. But as death tolls mounted, religious belief regained a large place in the private and public lives of Americans. Women and men mourning lost loved ones turned to prayer. Soldiers on both sides flocked to open-air religious services. Roughly two thousand chaplains enlisted in the Union Army, and hundreds of other benevolent volunteers distributed religious tracts in the camps. Most churches supported the war effort, with many religious leaders becoming vociferous in declaring their patriotism. The leading Northern sects reported increased membership over the war years.

The link between religion and patriotism took various forms. Certainly many observers had no trouble seeing Southern slaveholders as essentially immoral, leading to the conclusion that God sided with the Union, especially when the Northern forces became an army of emancipation. For others it was enough to see the Confederacy as an affront to law and order. When New York's bishop John Hughes declared that Catholics would "fight to the death for support of the Constitution, the Government and the laws" he was offering just such a connection between religious faith and political stability.

There were exceptions to this commingling of war and religion. While many Northerners of pacifist leanings became caught up in patriotic enthusiasm others continued their principled objection to war in any form. Despite their strong abolitionist sympathies, many Quakers persisted in their pacifism while affirming their loyalty to the government. These policies prompted painful debate within Quaker meetings across the North as their young men risked censure by enlisting in the Union cause. With the advent of the draft, conscientious objectors became a federal problem. The government allowed Quakers and other conscientious objectors continued access to the commutation fee; but some individuals refused to submit to even this indirect support of the war effort.

As some Americans turned to religion, others strayed far from the path of righteousness. People at home had good reason to worry about the moral experiences of their loved ones in uniform. Soldiers wrote home of gambling, drink, and prostitutes who trailed after the army. The American Temperance Union, concerned over rising wartime drinking, flooded the camps with temperance tracts aimed specifically at young soldiers. When veterans returned home or visited strange cities they brought their vices with them. Writers to local newspapers complained when furloughed soldiers brought their military camp manners into more genteel settings. Although scholars disagree about the war's effect on overall crime rates, Eric Monkkonen found a "high degree of public disorder" in wartime cities. Philadelphia's arrest patterns do not indicate increases in wartime crimes, but citations for running "disorderly houses" jumped from 127 in 1860 to 251 in 1864, perhaps reflecting the demands of soldiers passing through town or returning home on furlough. New ordinances in Jacksonville, Illinois, gave the police expanded authority to battle the dens of sin frequented by young soldiers. Chicagoans complained of escalating prostitution, gambling, and related depravity, exacerbated by the infusion of Mississippi riverboat gamblers fleeing from the conquered South.

By the summer of 1861 the Civil War was already part of the fabric of everyday Northern life, personal and public experiences blending together. When troops left for the front, individual families lived their own small dramas within a world that routinized its public leave-takings. Patriotic celebrations like Washington's birthday and Independence Day took on a special meaning during wartime; but towns and cities across the North marked those days with time-honored rituals rather than crafting new ceremonies for unprecedented times. Funeral processions and other public obsequies do not seem to have evolved in form, but as deaths became commonplace only the war's most famous victims attracted the public's attention.

The pattern was one of disequilibrium, followed by adjustment and a return to something close to normalcy. Certainly there were exceptions. Individuals struggled over the war's larger meaning. Families were shattered by its destruction. But whereas the Confederacy faced severe dislocations, the Northern cultural world seemed able to absorb the war's blows while pressing on with the routines of everyday life.

6

Economic Adjustments

WHEN ABRAHAM LINCOLN called for half a million more men in the summer of 1861, the North faced a staggering logistical and economic task. How would these men be supplied? Where would the money come from? How would a nation with a tiny military and a relatively small federal bureaucracy meet these enormous challenges? Another set of issues involves the repercussions of these economic decisions. What was the impact of military spending on everyday life at home? How were the sacrifices and gains distributed?

The Civil War armies and navies required an astonishing array of materiel. In addition to arms and ammunition, soldiers needed uniforms, boots, blankets, tents, food, and a bewildering assortment of supplies. Armies on the move used animals, wagons, railroad cars, bridges, and boats of all shapes and sizes. In the first few months of war the North could rely on stockpiles in federal arsenals and the ad hoc measures of state and regimental quartermasters, but a sustained war effort required more organization. The job of organizing the Union's supply system fell to Quartermaster General Montgomery C. Meigs. Meigs, a master of efficiency who had orchestrated the construction of Washington's famed aqueduct, proved well suited to the task. Within a few months he had begun to impose order on the North's chaotic contracting system. Edwin M. Stanton, who replaced Simon Cameron as secretary of war, provided further assurance that Union operations would run smoothly.

By the winter of 1861–1862 the Union had developed a mixed system of supply that combined federal production and supervision with private enterprise. At the center of this system stood the three central supply depots in Philadelphia, Cincinnati, and New York. Federal agents in each location purchased raw materials for the production of uniforms and tents on site while contracting other work to private entrepreneurs. With the destruction of the arsenal at Harpers Ferry, Virginia, the Springfield Armory in Massachusetts was the government's only arms factory until the completion of a new small-arms factory in Rock Island, Illinois. To supplement the armory's modest output the War Department turned to independent contractors.

This mingling of federal manufacturing and private contracting was a central feature of the Union's supply system. Military officials may have dictated the demand for goods, but market forces often determined the actual producers and prices. Such reliance on private contractors opened the door for charges of war profiteering. Soldiers returned home from campaigns with tales of uniforms falling apart in the first rain. Outraged citizens charged manufacturers with hoarding war materials to be sold at grossly inflated prices. A *Harper's Magazine* article on "The Fortunes of War" assailed members of the "shoddy aristocracy" who had profited from the nation's misery. ("Shoddy," a term used to describe a type of cheaply made cloth, became the label applied to poor-quality goods of all sorts.) Several state and federal commissions investigated these charges and uncovered wide-ranging corruption, particularly in the Department of the West. But most of the worst misdeeds dated to the war's first year, before Secretary of War Stanton began requiring open bidding on all contracts.

Once the initial kinks had been hammered out, the

federal supply system produced the best-equipped army the world had ever known. But even at its best that system had holes. Heavy losses from disease and malnutrition testify to both ignorance and inefficiency. Private initiatives continued to fill the gaps. Independent sutlers followed the troops wherever they marched, hawking food, stationery, and the like. Agents from the United States Sanitary Commission and other organizations distributed packages of supplies to soldiers in the camps.

Confederate supply officers faced a much more difficult task. At the outset of the war the North had tremendous advantages in nearly all aspects of manufacturing, transportation, and even food production. At first the South hoped to rely on imports to fill the void, but the diplomatic might of "King Cotton" proved weaker than expected, and the Union blockade successfully cut off many of the South's links to the outside world. Thus the Confederacy had to expand its own manufacturing output.

Despite the states' rights philosophy that drove the South into war, the Confederate government paradoxically played a more direct role in military supply than did its Northern counterpart. Where the Union relied on private contractors, a lack of private industry forced the South to construct and run its own factories. The Confederacy also proved more aggressive in controlling and subsidizing private enterprise, directing the movements of railroads, and even impressing slaves for military work. Yet it seems clear that neither side willingly turned to federally controlled activities unless existing local and private institutions proved inadequate to the task.

Both sides faced a formidable task in paying for the war. In antebellum America the national government had only modest responsibilities and limited sources of revenue. Over the four prewar years federal expenditures totaled a mere $274 million, financed largely through tariffs and the sale of public lands. With the coming of war the federal budget jumped astronomically. Direct costs of the Northern war effort have been estimated at $2.3 billion, with the federal government paying $1.8 billion; the Confederacy spent just over $1 billion on the war (at all levels). To put it another way, the Union's expenditures on the war were equivalent to more than 70 *percent* of the North's share of the 1859 gross national product.

Broadly speaking, the two governments had three options in responding to these fiscal challenges. First, they could rely on some form of taxation. But while the nation had a history of tariffs and modest excise taxes, the citizenry remained passionately resistant to any form of federal income tax. A second option was to turn to borrowing. The great advantage of this choice was that it would pass some of the cost of the war on to future generations (in the form of interest on the debt). A final choice was to print money and declare it legal tender—a policy not without cost. The printing of currency not backed by specie would raise prices, thus financing the war effort through inflation. The fiscal choices made by the two governments reveal much about their priorities and their circumstances.

As soon as the war began, President Lincoln ordered Treasury Secretary Salmon P. Chase to begin taking steps to fund the conflict. Chase faced an economy that had barely recovered from the Panic of 1857 before being thrown into recession by the secession crisis. Ever since the Second Bank of the United States had fallen victim to Jacksonian Democrats, the nation's monetary system had been in the hands of state-chartered banks which issued a bewildering assortment of banknotes circulating at various discount levels. This system had worked well enough in peacetime, but it posed major obstacles for a wartime economy.

Chase initially turned to increased import fees, excise taxes, and the sale of government land, but soon he shifted his attention to the sale of bonds. Investors, both at home and abroad, purchased bonds that would be redeemed with interest when they reached maturity. In this fashion the North hoped to fund its war effort through a form of borrowing. But as 1861 came to a close, the Treasury faced a serious crisis. With the Union Army faring poorly on the battlefield, and with England and the United States deeply at odds over the seizure of Confederate agents from the British ship *Trent*, the nation appeared on the verge of financial chaos. Worried citizens stopped buying bonds and began hording gold and silver, seriously depleting reserves both in state banks and at the Treasury. On December 30, 1861, state banks and the Treasury suspended specie payments. For a time soldiers and contractors went without pay, and the Union's future seemed in doubt.

Congress responded with the revolutionary Legal Tender Act of February 1862. The Legal Tender Act provided for the issuance of $150 million in non–interest-bearing notes. Although not backed by gold or silver, these "greenbacks" were legal tender for all debts except import duties and interest on government loans. By issuing notes without the backing of specie, the government risked serious inflation. But the greenbacks provided the Northern economy with an added means of exchange, helping it weather the crisis. And in the meantime Grant's victories in the West and the cooling of the *Trent* episode provided Northern financiers with more reason for optimism.

While bond sales and greenbacks proved instrumental in financing the war, their success owed much to the Union's taxation legislation which—in addition to raising revenues—helped support the government's credibility while reducing the greenbacks' inflationary effect. In August 1861 Congress passed a 3 percent tax on incomes of more than eight hundred dollars, but it was a year before those funds were collected. The following July a new revenue measure expanded income taxes and added an assortment of other levies.

By late summer 1862 bond sales had dwindled. Secretary Chase turned to Philadelphia broker Jay Cooke to orchestrate a massive campaign to stimulate them. Under Cooke's direction, 2,500 agents canvassed homes nationwide, pitching bonds to ordinary citizens. This strategy, which anticipated the patriotic war bond drives of World Wars I and II, succeeded in drawing investment from nearly a million Americans, or roughly one in four Northern families. By buying bonds, Northerners felt an additional link with the war effort. Yet it appears that most war bonds ended up in the hands of banks and wealthy investors.

The final piece of Chase's financial program did not fall into place until midway through the war. As the scale of expenditures increased, the North's unstable currency and chaotic banking system proved a consistent obstacle and an annoying impediment to the sale of bonds. The National Banking Act of February 1863 (and legislation in June 1864) established a new system of national banks. State banks wishing to obtain national bank charters had to invest one-third of their capital in government bonds. They were then eligible to issue national bank notes redeemable in gold for up to 90 percent of the value of the bonds they held. At first the state banks were hesitant to join the national banking fold. Finally, in March 1865, Congress passed a 10 percent tax on all notes issued by state banks. This measure proved a sufficient incentive to drive most state banks into the new national banking system.

How did these various measures combine to pay the Union's bills? When all was said and done bond sales funded two-thirds of the North's military expenses. Various forms of wartime taxation funded 21 percent of the war's cost, and remaining costs were financed through inflation. By printing greenbacks the federal government caused an increase in prices, which had a measurable impact on the Northern economy. At their peak, prices rose to 80 percent above antebellum levels. Economists estimate that these inflationary measures, beginning with the Legal Tender Act, paid for roughly 13 percent of the war effort. The

North's successful use of bonds reflected a combination of Northern wealth and widespread faith in the nation's future.

The Confederacy faced a similar fiscal challenge with far fewer economic tools. When the war began the rebels owned only 30 percent of the nation's wealth and 21 percent of its banking assets. With the success of the embargo and the reduction of cotton production, Southern planters found themselves with little cash to invest in their war effort. To make matters worse, Southerners disliked taxation. At first Confederate Treasury Secretary Christopher Memminger hoped to fund the war through taxes, thus avoiding more inflationary measures. In 1861 the South passed a small tariff and a modest tax on real and personal property. Policymakers initially distributed the burden to the individual states to collect. Most states ignored the legislation's objectives by adopting some other measure—land sales or bonds, for example—to circumvent true taxation. Finally, in April 1863 the Confederacy turned in desperation to quite heavy income and excise taxes. But by the war's end these various revenue measures had yielded less than 5 percent of the South's eventual war costs. Bond sales held a particular appeal for Confederate citizens, but before long their available cash had dried up. The Confederacy managed to fund only 35 to 40 percent of its costs through bonds.

With taxation and bond sales unable to meet the price of war, the Confederacy came to rely on printed treasury notes. By the end of the war the central government had issued $1.5 billion in Confederate notes while many states added their own notes and dozens of individuals injected badly made counterfeit bills into the South's developing fiscal disarray. Confederate notes financed roughly 60 percent of the South's war effort, but not without a terrible inflationary cost. By January 1863 the Southern price index had risen 760 percent in only two years. At the war's conclusion prices had little meaning in many parts of the Confederacy, but the best estimates are that prices were *ninety-two times* their antebellum level.

The funding legislation passed by the war Congress raises a broader issue. How did wartime measures reshape the American economy? One long-standing interpretation is that the war was a triumph of industrial capitalism. For decades the intellectual heirs to Thomas Jefferson and Alexander Hamilton had battled over the constitutionality of federal measures to assist economic development. With the Confederate congressmen safely out of the way—so the interpretation goes—Republicans were free to pursue an agenda which featured protective tariffs and strong banking legislation. The Civil War provided the perfect excuse for imposing a broad economic revolution.

In terms of the legislation adopted, this interpretation has much validity. Congressional voting on wartime economic measures divided along party lines as Democrats questioned the constitutionality, the economic wisdom, and even the morality of such initiatives. The Legal Tender Act passed with Republicans voting 3 to 1 in favor while Democrats lined up 3 to 1 against. The roll call on the National Banking Act yielded an even starker contrast—78 percent of Republicans in favor and 91 percent of Democrats opposed. In some cases the Republican platform coincided with war-related goals. Thus, shortly after taking office in 1861 the 37th Congress passed a protective tariff. In raising the tariff over the next several years it protected manufacturing while generating revenues. The Republicans' legislative agenda also went beyond these military measures. During the war years they passed the Homestead Act, providing 160 acres of public land to western settlers; the Morrill Land Grant College Act; and legislation assisting the transcontinental railroad. Before the war each of these measures had fallen victim to sectional or party conflict. Congress also voted to establish the National Academy of Sciences to aid technological development; the Department of Agriculture; the

Bureau of Printing and Engineering; and the Office of Comptroller of Currency. But recent scholarship has raised questions about the long-term significance of these measures.

Throughout the first half of the nineteenth century the American economy had been evolving from a very localized world, with little trade between regions, to an increasingly interdependent system. Textile firms in Massachusetts and Pennsylvania depended on Southern cotton crops; Southern planters relied on loans from Northern financiers; New England shoe factories produced for Southern markets. Thus the secession crisis sent a destabilizing shudder through the Northern economy. Some firms feared the loss of vital markets, others struggled as they were unable to collect on Southern debts. Investors viewed the crisis with cautious uncertainty. Shortly after Lincoln's election the economy plunged into depression. In January 1861 R. G. Dun and Company reported 859 business failures, more than twice the figure of the previous January. Unemployment jumped as demand for goods withered.

But these difficulties did not last long. By early 1862 recovery was well underway. Only 1,652 Northern businesses failed in 1862, nearly 4,300 fewer than in the preceding year. In the next three years R. G. Dun and Company reported a *total* of only 1,545 failures. The economy neared full employment as the North returned to prosperity.

What explains this rapid turnaround? Certainly the sudden demand for military goods provided an important stimulus. At the same time higher tariffs helped local manufacturing battle foreign competition. The administration's fiscal policies also aided the recovery. The printing of greenbacks provided a critical expansion of the money supply; wartime inflation eased the burden on debtors, enabling some merchants and manufacturers to expand their activities; and as the crisis ebbed, bankers provided firms with easier credit. At bottom the North's return to prosperity partly reflected its great economic might and the wide-spread confidence that the nation would ultimately prevail.

Different sectors of the Northern economy had different experiences. Some firms simply shifted their peacetime output to meet military demands, providing soldiers with the same goods they had previously sold to civilians. Others retooled factories to meet new needs: pitchfork manufacturers began producing swords; carpet makers sold army tents; one Philadelphia chandelier works began making cavalry spurs.

Textile manufacturers enjoyed heavy demand for tents and uniforms, but they had to overcome the lost access to Southern cotton. Although most successfully shifted their operations to woolen manufacturing, the war years saw an overall decline in textile production. New England's shoe factories stopped shipping roughly made shoes to slave plantations and began producing boots for military consumption. Shoe manufacturing, like textiles, experienced a net decline in total output during the war; but some scholars contend that the military demand, coupled with wartime labor shortages, helped accelerate the industry's use of technology and thus the rise of large shoe factories. Although some firearms firms prospered, munitions production overall did not expand over the war decade. Even output at the Du Pont explosives works grew less rapidly during the war than in previous years.

The Northern railway system played a key role in the Union's success. Here, as with military contracting, the government was generally content to rely on market forces. Although Congress gave Lincoln authority to take control of railroad lines for military necessity, he rarely exercised this power. In fact the Confederate government became much more involved in running Southern railroads. (But the threat of a federal imposition certainly aided the Union in negotiating rates with private companies.) The heavy demands on Northern railroads did not translate into substantial wartime growth. Rather than laying new track, railroad companies concentrated on replacing existing rails. And despite this demand for rails, pig iron production grew at the lowest rate since the War of 1812. Perhaps the Civil War's greatest impact on the nation's railroads was the impetus for a standard gauge. Before the war at least eleven different gauges were in use, creating enormous difficulties when troops tried to move from one line to another. On Quartermaster General Meigs's instigation, the railway companies made major strides toward adopting a single gauge.

Although we tend to think of the mid-nineteenth century as a time of rising industrialization, the fact is that the North, like the South, remained largely agricultural. In the antebellum decades Northern agriculture developed at a steady pace. Productivity increased as farmers invested in new technology; profits rose as improved transportation carried crops to far-off markets. The Civil War both stimulated and disrupted this process of development. The military had a voracious appetite for both food and animals, but the conflict also cut off trade with the South and siphoned off a disproportionate share of agricultural workers. The passage of the Homestead Act amplified this labor shortage by luring workers to try independent farming. Meanwhile, crop failures in western Europe stimulated a rising overseas demand for America's agricultural output. Overall the pace of agricultural mechanization increased as farmers turned to new machinery to offset labor shortages. But it appears that the growth in total agricultural output slowed during the war years and then burgeoned—at least in wheat and corn—after 1866. Producers of canned foods enjoyed a particular wartime boom which left a lasting mark on the American food industry. One of the most important regional developments was the rise of Chicago as the Midwest's dominant city. In the antebellum years Chicago had competed with St. Louis in grain sales while it vied with Cincinnati to be the nation's meat-packing capital. With the advent of war its chief competitors suffered the strains of lost Southern ties, leaving Chicago—which looked more east than south—free to prosper.

Despite dramatic shifts and substantial military demands, the war's economic impact on most sectors of the Northern economy was surprisingly slight and generally negative. Even where output expanded, it rarely matched the antebellum pace of growth. In some areas—agriculture and shoe manufacturing, for example—wartime labor shortages appear to have accelerated the level of mechanization. But on the whole the war seems to have had only a negligible effect on technological development, in either military or nonmilitary production.

The aggregate economic patterns mask a great variety of individual experiences. At one end of the spectrum a handful of wartime entrepreneurs parlayed military contracting into great wealth. Philip Armour made $2 million selling pork to the army; Clement Studebaker began amassing a fortune providing the Union with wagons; Andrew Carnegie traded in iron. But these men were the exception. Although many Northerners suspected that a class of unscrupulous businessmen was growing fat off the nation's despair, the impact of military contracting was generally broad rather than deep. Records of contracts signed in Philadelphia indicate that a wide range of companies provided military goods, many of them filling only an occasional order. The lure of government dollars generally appealed most powerfully to firms weakened by the secession crisis rather than to well-established companies. Thus war contracting probably had only a modest effect on the overall distribution of wealth.

For working-class men and women the Civil War created both opportunities and frustrations but few long-term changes. The secession crisis forced thousands of laborers out of work; when the economy recovered unemployment fell sharply. Although jobs were readily available, laborers did not share equally in the mid-war prosperity. Wage increases rarely kept pace with inflation, resulting in a steady decline in real wages, especially for unskilled workers. Part of this decline reflected shifts in the composition of the labor force as women, children, and unskilled immigrants replaced men who had gone to war. But clearly all laborers bore the brunt of wartime inflation. They countered by organizing and demanding higher pay.

In the antebellum years labor unions rose and fell with the state of the economy, with workers in the most skilled crafts leading the way. The secession crisis crippled most local unions and killed off all but three of the surviving nationals. When the nation returned to prosperity, unions reappeared in cities and towns across the North. National unions formed, new labor newspapers began publishing, and soon strikes became almost commonplace. In 1864, the year inflation reached its height, there were forty-two trade-wide strikes in New York City alone. These efforts yielded mixed results. Workers in the more skilled crafts sometimes managed to win concessions, but the vast majority of wage earners remained unorganized and ill equipped to battle union-busting employers.

In a few instances the army—claiming military necessity—stepped in to help employers battle workers. In March 1864 troops broke up a strike at the Parrott gun factory in Cold Spring, New York. The military temporarily seized control of the Reading Railroad when its engineers went on strike. Occasionally labor leaders who advocated draft resistance were placed under military arrest. But these episodes were the exception. More often employers acted alone or together to quash union activity through the use of scab labor and national blacklists. In 1864 *Chicago Times* publisher Wilbur F. Storey defeated striking typographers by hiring forty young women as printers and paying them 25 percent less than the men until the union caved in.

Overall the Civil War did little to transform most workers' experiences. Agricultural laborers continued to perform familiar tasks, though with some increased mechanization. Despite a scattering of large factories, most manufacturing workers labored in small shops organized along traditional lines. Even the emergence of unions and strikes followed familiar paths. Through it all, Northern workers only rarely exhibited an expanding sense of class consciousness. The combined forces of religion, culture, race, and gender kept workers from consistently finding common cause with other wage earners, even in the face of seemingly class-based conscription legislation.

Women have often found unusual economic opportunities in times of war. The Civil War increased the demand *for* women while placing uncommon demands *on* them, thereby shaping the wartime experience of women in both North and South.

When hundreds of thousands of men marched off to war, employers turned to women to help fill the gap. In agriculture women and children (as well as new machinery) offset the loss of perhaps a million male farm laborers. Women had held roughly a quarter of all manufacturing jobs in 1860; during the war that figure jumped to one-third. But these were not an earlier generation of "Rosie the Riveters," moving into new branches of heavy industry. Most women in government contracting turned to familiar female occupations in textiles, shoe manufacturing, and the like.

The seamstresses' plight reflects the dominant experience of female war workers. When the military arsenals first advertised for sewing women, mobs of job seekers crowded the gates competing for positions. Even after the economy improved, thousands of poor women—including growing numbers of war widows—remained desperate for work. Thus ruthless subcontractors could cut the already low piece rates for sewing work even as prices rose, so that sewing women worked longer hours for lower pay. Mass meetings in several cities called for improved conditions. In 1863 New

York's sewing women formed the Workingwomen's Protective Union to air their grievances. Philadelphia's seamstresses twice petitioned Abraham Lincoln for relief. But although the president agreed to order increased wages at the federal arsenals, most female workers remained at the mercy of subcontractors who enjoyed a surplus of available labor.

While most women toiled at familiar tasks, some blazed new trails. A handful found work in munitions. The removal of men accelerated the movement of women into the teaching profession; the enlistment of male clerks opened the door to office work. By 1865 447 women had won federal government jobs in Washington, D.C. The most dramatic changes came in nursing. As superintendent of the North's female nurses, Dorothea Dix proved instrumental in opening the profession to women while establishing rigorous standards. Under Dix's administration 3,200 female nurses served the Union Army, and thousands of others worked in hospitals and on battlefields for private relief agencies.

Even as the war presented women with new job opportunities, it also posed economic challenges at home. In the Confederacy the war's hardships, coupled with the large proportion of white males off in the army, brought Confederate women increased autonomy. Northern women faced fewer economic difficulties and perhaps proportionally less opportunity for autonomous action.

In the rural North, women took to the fields when men left for the front. One New York woman and her seven daughters ran a hundred-acre wheat farm that included twenty-two cows. In towns and cities, women whose husbands had enlisted ran businesses, managed family finances, and took on other traditionally male roles. But these changes should not be exaggerated. On the one hand, antebellum women had long been involved in running shops, managing boardinghouses, and directing other entrepreneurial activities, either as widows or alongside their husbands. On the other hand, even where men entered the army they did not necessarily leave their wives in complete control. Correspondence between soldiers and their wives reveals numerous cases of women exercising increased economic autonomy, but often husbands tried to assert their authority from a distance. Men in both the North and South turned to male friends and family members to "look after" family affairs in their absence.

The absence—and worse, the loss—of their male breadwinners was a blow for many women and children. The number of children in New York City's almshouse jumped by 300 percent during the war. Officials in both Boston and New York reported increases in juvenile delinquency, particularly among the youthful relatives of soldiers. In 1858 only 970 of 2,564 vagrants in Philadelphia's House of Correction were women; in 1863—a year in which the overall economy was much stronger—1,152 of Philadelphia's 1,697 vagrants were women. In 1860 women comprised only a fifth of the prisoners in Massachusetts jails; four years later that figure had jumped to 60 percent. But if the composition of the North's needy shifted toward women and children, the total drain on public and private benevolence dropped as the nation prospered.

The Civil War challenged the economic roles of women, but generally the adjustments were modest and short-lived. Apart from expansions in nursing, teaching, and civil service work, the lasting impact on female occupations was slight. When the men returned home, the percentage of women in manufacturing dropped to its antebellum level. If there was any wartime legacy to changes in private economic roles, it is harder to gauge. During the war wives took on additional tasks "for the duration." We can only wonder how they coped with the restoration of familiar roles when their husbands returned home.

The Civil War thus forced the North into economic adjustments at all levels of life. Government officials turned to new measures to raise funds and outfit the hastily created armies. Entrepreneurs shifted their operations to meet the demands of quartermasters. Working-class men and women sought employment with government contractors. Soldiers' families took on new economic responsibilities while their loved ones were at war. But these adjustments left the essential structure of the Northern economy largely unchanged. Financing and contracting relied on private enterprise rather than on public coercion. Most laborers, whether or not they were engaged in war production, experienced little change in the nature of their work.

Before the war the Northern economy was well on the path to industrialization. Rapid growth and development in mechanization, transportation, and communication had outstripped the Southern economy. During the war years these trends continued, though at a reduced rate. Investment in new structures and equipment slowed. Total output in agriculture and manufacturing continued to grow, but not as fast.

Setting the North's economic performance against that of the Confederacy, the contrast is clear. Total income in the South dropped dramatically, reflecting the combined weight of destruction, disrupted trade, and lost manpower. The North, in contrast, managed to fight the war without rationing, price controls, major shortages, or runaway inflation. And other than a few destructive rebel raids into Union territory, citizens in the North outside the border states escaped the devastation that ravaged the South.

7

Patriotic Adjustments

MOST NORTHERNERS who did not serve in uniform felt compelled to aid the war effort in some other way. In the first weeks of war patriotic citizens threw themselves into a flurry of activity, revealing more passionate enthusiasm than practical planning. After First Bull Run local and national voluntary societies eased into more carefully constructed routines, reflecting their understanding that this would be a long conflict. And these societies in turn reflected antebellum patterns of behavior and organizational standards, along with new adaptations to the circumstances of the war.

When the French aristocrat Alexis de Tocqueville traveled through the United States in the 1830s he was struck by the American penchant for voluntary associations. The second quarter of the nineteenth century witnessed an explosion in voluntary societies, particularly in the Northern states. New religious sects emerged; fraternal organizations flourished; labor unions ebbed and flowed. At the heart of all this activity was an impressive array of groups dedicated to reforming a society in constant flux. They met to battle alcohol, prostitution, and a litany of sins. Other organizations dedicated themselves to aiding widows, orphans, and the poor. The most numerous and energetic societies formed in opposition to slavery.

These antebellum voluntary societies produced a dense web of associations, reflecting the diversity of American culture. Many were affiliated with specific churches; others adopted vague Christian rhetoric; still others insisted on militant nonsectarianism. Most organizations grew from local roots. But in some cases—the American Anti-Slavery Society, for instance—national bodies emerged to provide local chapters with philosophical underpinnings and strategic direction. Women dominated the rank and file in most benevolent associations, but men often held the powerful offices. Thus male managers directed organizations dedicated to urban poor relief, but they often relied on the opinions of female "visitors" when dispensing funds. At abolitionist meetings male speakers dominated podiums before predominantly female audiences.

The varied demands of the Civil War produced a similarly diverse collection of patriotic organizations, ranging from the nationwide activities of the passionately efficient United States Sanitary Commission to a number of neighborhood bodies dedicated to helping men in a single local hospital. At first this enthusiasm yielded some spectacularly foolish results, as when sewing circles flooded camps with "havelocks" —kepis with flaps in the back to keep off the sun—that were better suited to desert warfare; or when groups of women worked diligently scraping lint for hospitals, only to discover that readily available machinery could do the task in a fraction of the time. Soon individuals and groups learned to navigate the war's complex demands, and an intricate, multitiered voluntaristic structure evolved.

Shortly after the war began a group of women from New York City's elite families formed the Woman's Central Association of Relief to assist government authorities in bringing the troops medical aid. A few weeks later New York minister Dr. Henry W. Bellows, inspired by the Woman's Central Association, led a delegation to Washington to lobby for improved sanitation and medical care in the camps. In June 1861 the group received official status as the

United States Sanitary Commission, charged with inspecting the camps, collecting medical supplies, and advising a somewhat reluctant Medical Bureau. President Lincoln accepted the plan with some skepticism, fearing that the USSC would become the "fifth wheel on the coach." Soon Bellows and his followers stood atop a national voluntaristic empire, with seven thousand local auxiliaries actively raising funds and funneling donated food, medicine, and clothing to ten regional depots. The Sanitary Commission sent paid agents into the field to visit the troops, distribute goods, and inspect sanitary and medical conditions in the camps.

Later in 1861 YMCA officials launched the United States Christian Commission, yet another national organization for soldiers' relief. The USCC shared much in common with the larger Sanitary Commission. Both voluntary bodies relied on local affiliates to collect money and goods to be delivered to the camps. But their differences were clear and widely publicized. Whereas the Sanitary Commission rejected all religious influences in favor of highly efficient, scientific management, the Christian Commission dispensed bibles and religious tracts along with material goods. And while the Sanitary Commission relied on professional, paid agents, the Christian Commission depended on unpaid volunteers. Despite occasional public sparring, the two national commissions were essentially similar in their reliance on a national, bureaucratic structure dominated by elite white men. They also set the North apart from the Confederacy, which never developed any similarly large voluntaristic organizations.

The national voluntary commissions were only the tip of the Civil War's benevolent iceberg. In towns and cities across the North, citizens came together in hundreds of small organizations wherever they saw a need. Many local groups worked alongside the Sanitary Commission and the Christian Commission in sending aid to soldiers in the field. Patriotic women formed sewing circles that met several times a week. Soldiers' Aid Societies collected money and prepared packages of clothing, bandages, and food. In their first year of operation the Ladies' SAS of Springfield, Illinois, distributed 50 cotton shirts, 522 cotton drawers, and 155 pairs of slippers as well as socks, handkerchiefs, towels, pillowcases, bandages, and a wide assortment of food to soldiers in the field. These community groups generally earmarked their contributions to local regiments, thus maintaining their personal connection with home-town troops. Some local bodies eventually affiliated with the Sanitary Commission, but others sent their own agents into the field, completely circumventing any national direction. Nor did the Christian Commission monopolize the religious effort. Tract societies scattered throughout the North shipped their own pamphlets to war-weary troops. The New York Bible Society, in its fourth decade when the war began, distributed more than 85,000 volumes to 139 regiments in 1861 alone. And Catholic nuns from the Sisters of Mercy became a familiar sight in the Union's military camps.

Other societies dedicated themselves to helping men closer to home. As wounded soldiers recuperated in Northern hospitals, small groups of benevolent women, often from a particular city ward or church congregation, organized into teams of visitors to read to patients, help them send letters home, and generally provide care and comfort. In response to the disabled and unemployed veterans who began appearing on city streets, voluntary societies opened forty Soldiers' Homes which combined to provide 4.5 million meals and a million nights' lodging for needy men. Soldiers' Reading Rooms were established to serve those men who simply wanted a place to relax and perhaps enjoy a hot meal.

Philadelphia's refreshment saloons are a clear example of the North's decentralized voluntarism in action. Soldiers arriving by steamboat in the City of Brotherly Love often had to wait several hours in the southern part of town before boarding southbound trains. Local women, seeing these hungry troops, began bringing them coffee and sandwiches. Soon two voluntary institutions, the Cooper Shop Refreshment Saloon and the Volunteer Refreshment Saloon, formed to organize these activities and raise money to fund future efforts. Men and women from the neighborhood ran both organizations. Together they provided 1.3 million meals to passing soldiers. With time both expanded their services to include facilities for men who were unable to continue on their journey. Although the two refreshment saloons performed identical tasks in buildings virtually across the street from each other, they never combined their activities. Their only concession to central control was formally to agree to take turns greeting incoming regiments. Instead they persisted as highly independent, localized bodies reflecting complex associational webs rather than abstract theories about organization and efficiency.

Still more local groups formed to assist the war's other victims. In many cities and towns private groups worked alongside city officials to raise funds to distribute to the families of volunteers. Quakers were particularly troubled by any action that might indirectly assist the war effort. Some attracted notoriety by knitting soldiers' mittens without trigger fingers. Soon they found outlets for their benevolence that did not compromise principles. Many became active in raising money and providing assistance to the flood of contrabands—runaway slaves—who fled North. Northern free blacks were active in assisting contrabands, sending aid to enclaves of Southern freedpeople, and, eventually, preparing packages for local black regiments. Chicagoans brought food and warm clothing to Southern prisoners held in Camp Douglas. After Confederate troops burned Chambersburg, Pennsylvania, citizens across the region formed spontaneous organizations to collect donations. In a particularly interesting case of benevolence, when they learned that the Civil War had crippled the British cotton textile industry, Philadelphians raised money to send to Manchester's impoverished factory workers.

The North's array of benevolent organizations is perhaps most remarkable in its diversity. Following a process that Tocqueville would certainly have recognized, groups of concerned individuals responded to new problems by calling public meetings, forming societies, electing officers, and setting about making their own small contribution. This pattern duplicated itself in cities and towns throughout the North, though different locations responded to their own circumstances and traditions. The older Eastern cities were best situated to adapt established neighborhood, ethnic, religious, and class associations to the new demands. One historian has suggested that Chicago, a much younger city, could not long sustain such ad hoc local groups. Instead philanthropic Chicagoans threw themselves into making their city the hub of the Sanitary Commission's Northwestern branch.

One effect of this institutional complexity was that prospective volunteers were free to do as much or as little as they chose. At one end of the spectrum were men and women who volunteered to travel into the field as agents for local or national groups. Some of these people toiled in anonymity; others became household names. Immediately after the war several popular books memorialized the heroic sacrifices of the North's most active women. At home hundreds of individuals immersed themselves in organizing war work. Collectively these leaders looked very much like antebellum America's "benevolent empire," which had been comprised of a highly moral core of conservative middle- and upper-class men and women, many of whom had served on the boards of several different philanthropic bodies. But the array of organizations opened the doors to new activists, including some from more modest circumstances.

Beneath the philanthropic leadership were the mass of patriotic volunteers. As in antebellum organizations, even where the officers were men, most of the rank and file were women. Their diaries and letters reveal the ways in which Northern women wove voluntary activity into the fabric of their daily wartime lives. In a typical week an unmarried woman might spend one evening at a sewing circle, a second evening attending a Soldiers' Aid Society meeting, an afternoon reading to men at the local hospital, and several more hours visiting the wives of men who had enlisted. Others remained far less involved but were ready to lend assistance after a major battle or during an important fund-raising drive. Often the personal and patriotic became intertwined, as when young women sewed garments for friends and loved ones in the field. Even when they worked for the highly impersonal Sanitary Commission, the volunteers managed to put a distinctive mark on their efforts. One woman delivered a large package of cookies to the Sanitary Commission's Chicago depot with a warning note attached: "These cookies are expressly for the sick soldiers, and if anyone else eats them, *I hope they will choke him!*"

The history of wartime medicine brings together many of the central aspects of the Civil War experience, including both strong continuities and important adjustments. Twice as many Civil War soldiers died of disease as from battle wounds. Several forces combined to create this sad record. Recruits received almost no medical examination before entering the army. Camp life not only exposed them to harsh routines and filthy conditions, it also put men from diverse disease environments in close proximity. Ironically, hardy farm boys who had never left their home county fared far worse than less vigorous-looking urban factory workers who had spent a lifetime exposed to contagious disease. Those who fell ill or received wounds faced primitive treatment that may have done more harm than good. But the fact is that even the best medical minds knew little of the importance of bacteria in spreading disease, or the value of antiseptics. And as abysmal as medical treatment may have been, Civil War volunteers fared better than soldiers in earlier wars.

The Medical Bureau oversaw medical treatment in the Union Army. When the war began the surgeon general, an aging veteran of forty-three years of military service, resisted progressive ideas and battled the encroachments of the Sanitary Commission's civilian interlopers. But in April 1862 neurologist William Hammond, a much younger man, took over the position, and the bureau began to work more closely with the USSC's agents. Meanwhile, the number of army doctors grew from 113 in 1860—two dozen of whom resigned to serve the Confederacy—to a total of fifteen thousand who served the two armies throughout the war.

The history of Northern hospitals is yet another example of a development combining public and private initiatives. On the battlefields surgeons worked in hospital tents or in nearby buildings commandeered for the purpose. Wounded soldiers who were far from home received treatment in floating hospital ships. Once they had returned to the North many men ended up in private hospitals that had been given over to military work. New York City aldermen arranged to take over buildings of Mount St. Vincent Academy in Central Park to serve as an emergency hospital. With time the federal government supplemented these existing hospitals with a network of large general hospitals. But even these sprawling federal hospitals welcomed the efforts of private volunteers.

Despite enormous energy devoted to the care of wounded soldiers, the Civil War generated surprisingly few medical advances. Philadelphian Silas Wier Mitchell, one of postwar America's leading surgeons, made important strides in his study of the neurological trauma accompanying gunshot wounds. The North pioneered a new pavilion design for hospitals that maximized the free circulation of fresh air. And in perhaps the most important new initiative, the

Union Army, responding to pressures from the Sanitary Commission, developed the use of a trained ambulance corps. Still, after four years of war surgeons knew little more about medical treatment than they had at First Bull Run.

Although the quality of medical care did not evolve very quickly, the Civil War saw important changes in the roles of women in the nursing profession. Before the war it was commonly assumed that the grisly scenes of a hospital were inappropriate sights for properly modest women. It was one thing to allow ladies to visit men to soothe a forehead, read a letter, and generally provide comfort and good cheer, but only men had been allowed to serve as nurses. Shortly before the Civil War Florence Nightingale had challenged these assumptions in the Crimea. Dorothea Dix, a well-known reformer for the treatment of the mentally ill, became the Union Army's superintendent of female nurses. Dix created high standards of professionalism and strict entrance requirements intended to protect the reputations of her corps of female nurses. Applicants were to be plain-looking women over the age of thirty who would attract no improper attention from the wounded men. Walt Whitman, who served in Washington as a nurse, agreed with such rigid rules. "Few or no *young* ladies," he reasoned, "under the irresistible conventions of society, answer the practical requirements of nurses for soldiers."

By the end of the war 3,200 women—one-quarter of all nurses—served the Union Army, and thousands more acted as volunteers. Harriet Douglas Whetten, a Sanitary Commission nurse from Staten Island, worked on a hospital ship during McClellan's failed 1862 Peninsular Campaign. In one letter home Whetten described a colleague as "too fine a lady to make a good nurse, [she] touches things somewhat too much with the tips of her fingers, so that the actual nursing in our ward falls chiefly to me." But in the same note she added, "You must understand that there are men nurses and orderlies detailed, so that we volunteer ladies have nothing disagreeable to do." Clearly Whetten envisioned female nurses filling a particular niche rather than duplicating the work of the men. By the time she returned home the weary veteran had little patience for dilettantish ladies. When the hospital ship reached home she wrote, "The usual crowd of patriotic Philadelphia females assembled and insisted upon feeding our boys, pouring their stuff into the eyes and noses of such as were on stretchers, and insisting upon drenching a young nurse."

Although these female nurses blazed new trails and changed attitudes along the way, they did not do so without resistance. General Ulysses S. Grant blocked his wife Julia's desire to do hospital work. Other men wrote home warning wives of the unflattering comments made by soldiers about volunteer nurses. Disgruntled nurses described arrogant male doctors refusing to let them do the jobs for which they were trained. The handful of female doctors faced even more difficult obstacles. Dr. Esther Hill Hawks ended up teaching freedmen in the South when she was unable to find an opportunity to perform her craft. Dr. Emily Blackwell, one of the nation's leading female physicians, was instrumental in starting New York's Women's Central Association but could not win a major position in the Medical Department.

While legions of volunteers threw themselves into philanthropic work, other Northerners grappled for the public mind. Some of these efforts followed normal partisan routes. Politicians and party leaders contested local and national elections as they had in peacetime; newspaper editors used their pages to celebrate or excoriate the latest policies. But the Civil War also saw the development of sophisticated propaganda techniques offered in the name of patriotism. At the center of it all was a flood of printed pamphlets.

Pamphleteering had a long tradition in Anglo-American politics. American Revolutionaries borrowed their pamphleteering techniques from an earlier generation of British opposition writers. In the antebellum decades reformers took advantage of reduced publication costs to bring their case to more citizens via the printed word. Antislavery activists used their enormous network of local auxiliaries to distribute abolitionist tracts to an eager audience; missionary tract societies dispensed religious materials far and wide. But if Civil War pamphleteers did not invent their craft, they certainly elevated it to a higher level.

During the first two years of the war the publication of pamphlets remained scattered and localized. But by the war's second winter partisans on all sides felt an increasing need to bring their case to the public. In February 1863 a group of self-styled loyal Democrats, led by leading lawyer Samuel Tilden and financier August Belmont, met at Delmonico's Restaurant in New York and founded the Society for the Diffusion of Political Knowledge. The group elected Samuel Morse as their president and set about publishing pamphlets attacking the Lincoln administration's policies as unconstitutional. The following day another group of New Yorkers responded with its own Loyal Publication Society. And before a week was out Philadelphia's Union League created a separate Board of Publications. The Society for the Diffusion of Political Knowledge printed more than a hundred different pamphlets in the next two years. The Loyal Publication Society countered by distributing 900,000 copies of ninety patriotic pamphlets. The Union League printed an astonishing four million copies of its 104 pro-Republican publications. One Democrat complained, "You can hardly go into a public office or store but you will see...[Union League] documents on tables, counters, and even *posted* as handbills."

This explosion of pamphlets certainly did not produce a balanced dialogue. Proadministration forces had far more resources at their disposal. But unlike normal partisan debates, the intention was not only to garner votes but to kindle patriotic enthusiasm after long months of war. Thus many Union pamphlets cultivated anti-Southern feeling rather than merely generating pro-Republican sentiment. The pamphlets are also noteworthy in their range of topics and anticipated audiences. Sometimes the Society for the Diffusion of Political Knowledge took the high ground, making complex arguments on the writ of habeas corpus and similar issues. On other occasions it appealed to readers' baser fears with publications such as "Miscegenation Indorsed by the Republican Party." Propagandists on both sides targeted particular groups by publishing materials in different languages as well as pamphlets directed specifically at workers or women. And while many publications tackled the intricate policy issues of the day, others were calculated to raise popular ire with vivid accounts of Southern atrocities.

Civil War pamphlets may have been aimed at a very broad readership, but the men who controlled the printing presses represented no such cross section. The publication societies and the Union Leagues were controlled by powerful white men with financial resources who sought to influence the nation's future. Their labors reflect both the importance of private voluntarism and the ongoing power of the Northern elites.

Pamphleteers were not, however, the North's most adept propagandists. That title must certainly go to Abraham Lincoln himself. From early in his career Lincoln recognized the importance of public opinion. During the war he took pains to mold popular thought by sending open letters to newspapers, working closely with the ostensibly independent Union Leagues, and carefully crafting his own speeches to reach the broadest possible audience.

As powerful as printed words were, the Northern mood may have been as significantly affected by public displays in the streets. Throughout the nineteenth century various groups competed for control of shared public space. Often civic holidays, such as Independence Day and George Washington's birthday, became occasions for local political and military leaders to assert their status through organized parades while members of the working classes engaged in nights of spontaneous revelry. With the outbreak of war the central dates on the patriotic calendar took on new meaning. The Fourth of July, the day set aside for enthusiastic nationalism, became a particular object of attention.

In peacetime Northern communities commemorated the nation's birthday with picnics, parades, and patriotic oratory followed by evenings lit by fireworks. Through four long years of war Northerners continued to mark Independence Day in familiar fashion. Often the amount and nature of public display reflected the progress on the battlefield. When the news was good, flags and bunting hung over the streets and the pealing of bells filled the air. On other occasions parades and oratory seemed to exhort the citizenry to stay with the cause. On July 4, 1863, the day after the bloody Battle of Gettysburg, cities canceled their celebrations in favor of more contemplative ceremonies.

Given the symbolic value of Independence Day, the control of civic ritual could have taken on special meaning. Periodically Philadelphia's city officials discussed sponsoring large demonstrations, but time and again they abandoned such plans, preferring to devote tax dollars to more pragmatic concerns. Instead the day remained in the hands of private citizens who often staged enormous displays. Springfield, Illinois, a town torn by partisan strife, commemorated July 4, 1861, with a huge procession after which all partisan toasting was banned. But for the next three years political and ethnic squabbling foiled all attempts to sponsor a single community-wide event. Only in July 1865 could Springfield manage to come together for a shared celebration.

In their eagerness to support the war effort, Northern women and men turned to their own experiences and traditions for guidance. Along the way they adjusted their methods, roles, and even ideologies, but through it all much remained consistent with antebellum practices.

The essential organization and operation of wartime philanthropies looked very much like those of their antebellum predecessors. In benevolent societies as in military companies, volunteers congregated by class, neighborhood, religion, and ethnic group. As in peacetime, much energy went into raising money to fund activities. Through most of the war the familiar devices proved sufficient. Newspapers regularly contained notices for fund-raising concerts, small "fancy fairs," or amateur theatricals to support the local refreshment saloon or Soldiers' Aid. The biggest change brought on by the war was in the sheer amount of benevolent activity. And even as new bodies formed to sew clothing, feed soldiers, visit hospitals, aid contrabands and refugees, and attend to a variety of other war-related challenges, the established charities carried on. Clearly the pull of patriotism led citizens to dig deeper into their pockets and sacrifice more of their time.

More innovative was the introduction of the two national groups, the Sanitary Commission and the Christian Commission. To be sure, antebellum Americans had had experience with national voluntary organizations. The American Anti-Slavery Society had branches across the North; local churches affiliated with national bodies; trade unions had already begun national cooperative efforts. But the operations of the two wartime commissions, and the Sanitary Commission in particular, went far beyond familiar practices. Under the direction of executive secretary Frederick Law Olmsted, the architect who had designed New York's Central Park, the Sanitary Commission's leadership proclaimed a deep passion for order and efficiency and insisted that those goals could be achieved only through careful, centralized control. But the question remains, How fully did this governing philosophy trickle down to the local auxiliaries? Citizens who joined local branches of a highly organized national body seemed to be adopting a nationalist strategy for fighting a nationalist war. But it is not at all clear that memoranda drafted in New York City had a powerful effect in the hinterlands. Volunteers continued to think in terms of local concerns even while attending Sanitary Commission functions. And even if the Sanitary Commission's leaders gained ideological converts among the rank and file, thousands of other volunteers worked in entirely autonomous groups.

The publication societies suggest a similar melding of the old and the new. While their strategy of distributing printed pamphlets to mold public opinion had deep historic roots, the patriotic societies took the nation onto new paths with the magnitude of their efforts.

Most important, the benevolent societies, the pamphleteers, and even the architects of civic ritual suggest a further continuity: all reveal the continued prominence of private activism. The Sanitary Commission enjoyed official sanction but not government control. At election time the publication societies worked hand-in-glove with the political parties but maintained a clear autonomy. Even though all agreed that morale was vital to military success, public officials generally left the funding and planning of civic rituals in private hands.

The war similarly failed to bring a dramatic change to the role played by women in the sphere of voluntary associations. In most of their wartime work women followed well-worn antebellum paths. Many smaller organizations— sewing circles or hospital visitation groups—were composed entirely of women, perhaps with a man as honorary treasurer. But where men and women served in the same organizations, the division of labor (and power) mirrored earlier experiences. Women made up the vital rank and file, but men consistently claimed the leading positions. Annual reports generally named the male officers first, followed by a list of "lady managers." This division was particularly true for the male-dominated national organizations. Of course such evidence can be deceptive. Even where male names appeared in places of prominence, female volunteers may have been making the vital day-to-day decisions. But this too continued established practice.

Some exceptions do suggest the unusual opportunities presented by the Civil War. Young women who rose to prominence in New York's Women's Central Association of Relief went beyond familiar practices in adopting the strategies and philosophies of the Sanitary Commission. In Chicago Mary Livermore and Jane C. Hoge became dominant figures in the USSC's Northwestern Branch. In the fall of 1863 they led a committee of women who staged a regional fair which earned $86,000 for the Sanitary Commission. Other women found expanded gender roles by resisting organizational hierarchies. Clara Barton established her own relief operation that anticipated the postwar Red Cross. But even where patriotic women earned wide recognition for their heroic sacrifices, most of their war work remained within the confines of accepted gender roles.

8

Racial Adjustments

AN UNDERSTANDING OF how the Civil War affected the North's racial world must begin with an underscoring of two important aspects of the situation when the war began. First, although slavery was behind most of the conflicts that led to the war, the North did not enter the Civil War with a goal of ending the South's peculiar institution. True, many individuals saw the fighting as the first step in an abolitionist crusade. But Abraham Lincoln was quick to insist that he was interested only in restoring the Union. To declare otherwise would have been to risk losing his tenuous hold on the border states as well as much of his support closer to home. Thus the Emancipation Proclamation represented a major shift in the Union's war aims.

Second, although many Northerners were opposed to slavery, very few embraced a philosophy of racial equality. Both law and local tradition made African Americans second-class citizens. The actual circumstances of black Northerners varied greatly from state to state. Black diarist Charlotte Forten, who attended an integrated school in Salem, Massachusetts, was often dismayed by the open racism she encountered when she returned home to Philadelphia. And in neighboring Delaware, slavery remained legal throughout the war.

From the outset the Radical Republicans wanted emancipation as a condition for returning the Southern states to the Union. But Lincoln refused to move too quickly. Although he personally opposed slavery, he was mindful that his victory margin had been small and that his best hopes for a hasty end to the conflict lay with Unionists in the border and Southern states. Better to wage war on the firmest constitutional grounds than to raise the slave issue prematurely.

When their moral and constitutional arguments failed to win converts, the abolitionists began to place emancipation under the banner of military necessity. In May 1861 three Virginia slaves escaped into Union hands at Fortress Monroe. General Benjamin Butler refused to return the runaways to their masters, declaring them "contraband of war." When news of this action reached the plantations, thousands more slaves fled into Union hands as "contrabands." That August Congress formalized this policy with legislation permitting the confiscation of all property, including slaves, that had been assisting the Confederate military. These early steps were still quite modest. They helped only those slaves who could somehow find their way to Union lines. And both Butler's proclamation and Congress's legislation continued to describe slaves as property.

On August 30 General John C. Frémont, the Union's commander in the West, issued a proclamation freeing all slaves held by Confederate sympathizers in Missouri. Lincoln quickly countermanded the flamboyant general's order, and from that moment Frémont's days in command were numbered. The following May the president drew fire from Radical Republicans when he revoked a similar order issued by General David Hunter emancipating all slaves in the "Department of the South." While willing to support emancipation out of military necessity, Lincoln resisted sweeping proclamations issued from below. Instead he hoped to solve his dilemma by convincing the loyal border states to accept voluntary emancipation. In March he proposed legislation offering financial inducements to slaveowners for gradual emancipation. Congress passed the bill along party lines, but border state representatives repeatedly rejected Lincoln's pleas for cooperation.

Meanwhile, pressure from Congress and the military mounted. In the absence of clear policy, Union generals treated the flood of contrabands in diverse ways, often reflecting their own political leanings. In July 1862 Congress passed its second confiscation act, permitting the seizure of property belonging to people in rebellion and specifically declaring that all slaves who reached Union lines would be freed. This legislation went well beyond earlier measures both in its breadth of coverage and in making explicit provision for the freeing of slaves. Still, the act placed the burden on authorities to determine if slaveowners were in fact in rebellion. Lincoln continued to have doubts about the constitutionality and political wisdom of the new confiscation act. In August he discussed his views in an open letter to the *New York Tribune*'s Horace Greeley, who had made repeated calls for immediate emancipation. "My paramount objective in this struggle," Lincoln explained, "is to save the Union, and is not either to save or to destroy slavery. If I could save the Union without freeing any slave I would do it, and if I could save it by freeing all the slaves I would do it; and if I could save it by freeing some and leaving others alone, I would also do that."

By the war's second summer Lincoln had already become convinced that emancipation in the Confederate states would be an extremely important war measure: it would seize enemy property while encouraging slaves to flee, and it would augment Union ranks. And he judged that the political climate would now support it. That August Senator John Sherman wrote to his brother, General William T. Sherman, from Ohio: "You can form no conception of the change of opinion here as to the Negro Question. Men of all parties who now appreciate the magnitude of the contest and who are determined to preserve the unity of the government at all hazards, agree that we must seek the aid and make it the interests of the negroes to help us." This, Sherman concluded, should include "the broad issue of universal emancipation." Senator Sherman did not know that Lincoln had already drafted his Emancipation Proclamation and was only awaiting a suitable victory to make it public.

Although the Battle of Antietam was no sweeping victory, it gave the president his opportunity. On September 22, 1862, Lincoln declared that as of January 1, 1863, all slaves in states still in rebellion would be "then, thenceforth, and forever free." Even with these revolutionary words Lincoln maintained his moderate stance. He issued this preliminary proclamation on strict military grounds in his capacity as commander-in-chief. (A broader decree would have required legislation.) The only slaves covered by the proclamation were those who were in enemy hands and thus outside of immediate Union influence. Meanwhile, slavery remained undisturbed in the border states as well as in conquered Confederate territory in Virginia, Louisiana, and Tennessee. Lincoln continued to hope that the loyal states would voluntarily accept gradual emancipation.

As he feared, Lincoln faced protests following the preliminary Emancipation Proclamation. Democrats exploited popular fears and hostility to win a series of state and national victories in the 1862 elections. Some Union soldiers declared they had no interest in dying to free slaves. The previous January one volunteer wrote home to his fiancée: "It is not for the emancipation of the African race I fight. I want nothing to do with the negro. I want them as far from me as is possible to conceive.... When President Lincoln declares the slaves emancipated I will declare myself no longer an American citizen." Working-class Northerners—and Irish immigrants in particular—worried about emancipation's implications as they envisioned thousands of free blacks flooding north to compete for precious jobs.

The Emancipation Proclamation was not as radical as some abolitionists would have liked, but it had an enormous impact on the Civil War's essential nature. After insisting for nearly two years that they were fighting only to restore the Union, the Northern military suddenly became an army of liberation. The *Springfield Republican* declared the preliminary proclamation "the greatest social and political revolution of the age." Although slaveholders in the occupied territories and border states could keep their slaves, they could see the handwriting on the wall. Foreign observers who had resisted taking sides in an internal dispute could now identify the North as firmly on the moral high ground. Free blacks who had doubted their interest in the conflict now rallied to the cause.

The resistance to emancipation, though substantial, was far less than it would have been only two years earlier. The Republicans lost ground in the 1862 elections, but if the elections were a referendum on the Emancipation Proclamation, the popular judgment was still favorable. Much of this shift reflected the growing belief that emancipation would help win the war.

Americans had historically accepted black soldiers only in times of crisis. Blacks served the United States in both the American Revolution and the War of 1812, but as soon as each war ended they were immediately disarmed. In fact in 1792 the new Congress formally banned blacks from the federal militia. Although some people feared armed insurrection if blacks were given weapons, most objections were based on racist assumptions about black inferiority. Critics claimed that blacks lacked the requisite discipline and courage to perform under fire. Moreover, military service, particularly in peacetime, was viewed as the purview of the elites.

How, they wondered, could a gentleman be expected to die honorably alongside, or at the hands of, his inferiors?

Before the Emancipation Proclamation, Abraham Lincoln repeatedly questioned the wisdom of allowing blacks to serve in uniform. On several occasions Union generals acted on their own to accept black enlistments, but each time they were overruled. Whatever military benefits they offered, Lincoln reasoned, were likely to be outweighed by political damage. But if prejudice kept blacks out of the army, the navy had no such immutable rules. Thousands of black Americans had already served at sea by 1863, and many of them had fought gallantly in combat. In the spring of 1862 Robert Smalls, a South Carolina slave, earned widespread fame by stealing the Confederate ship *Planter* and sailing it out of Charleston harbor into Union hands.

In July 1862 two pieces of legislation opened the doors for wider black participation in the military. The second confiscation act gave the president the power to use contrabands in any way he saw fit. And the Militia Act included provisions for enrolling blacks for military service. At first Lincoln was content to limit blacks to supporting positions as laborers and drivers, and in similar noncombatant roles. But even as he was maintaining such limits, Secretary of War Stanton was authorizing the enlistment of five thousand freed slaves in South Carolina.

With the issuance of the preliminary Emancipation Proclamation, popular discussion of black troops intensified. Some whites persisted in questioning whether blacks could be effective soldiers. Others welcomed the opportunity to fill military quotas without putting more whites at risk. Lincoln himself concluded that "whatever Negroes can be got to do as soldiers, leaves just so much less for white soldiers to do, in saving the Union." This, then, became the other half of his military necessity argument.

Within the African American community the prospect of emancipation brought an important shift in attitudes. Some

Northern blacks had been anxious to take up arms against the Confederacy from the outset. Even if the war was not yet being fought over slavery, they welcomed any opportunity to help defeat the hated slaveocracy. In the war's first months some formed companies and volunteered their services, only to be sent home in humiliation. Other black leaders argued they should have no part of this war. In late April 1861 Philadelphia's *Christian Recorder*, a leading black newspaper, declared that "to offer ourselves for military service *now, is to abandon self-respect* and *invite insult.*" New York's *Anglo-African* disagreed. "The South must be subjugated," it insisted in August 1861, "or we shall be enslaved." Thus the paper called on New York's blacks to prepare to be called. "Colored men whose fingers tingle to pull the trigger, or clutch the knife aimed at the slave-holders in arms, will not have to wait much longer," it promised.

When the Emancipation Proclamation took effect and barriers to black service fell, excited black volunteers enlisted with the same spirit that whites had shown after Fort Sumter. The most eager recruits signed up with three new regiments being formed in Massachusetts. Soon the War Department had approved regiments in cities and towns across the North. In many ways black recruiting followed a trajectory similar to white recruiting, but two years later. In the early months young volunteers clamored for available spaces. Before long the most willing recruits were already in uniform, and rumors of unfair treatment gave others pause. Local and federal recruiters countered with rallies, circulars, and eventually bounties, much as these strategies had been used to entice white volunteers. Many of the North's black leaders played crucial roles in this recruiting process. Ex-slaves Frederick Douglass and William Wells Brown served as paid recruiters, traveling throughout the North and stirring up enthusiasm. Local black elites helped with equal fervor. In May 1863 the African Methodist Episcopal Church in Philadelphia announced that "considered in the light of self-interest and mutual protection, it is the duty of the entire colored people of the North" to support the war with arms. By the end of the war 179,000 black men had served in 166 all-black regiments. Most of these soldiers were recently freed slaves, but more than 34,000 free Northern blacks also fought for the Union. In addition to these troops, perhaps 200,000 more blacks assisted the army in various support capacities.

Once they were allowed to fight, the performance of black soldiers took on great symbolic significance. Although black leaders celebrated the opportunities that would accompany military service, black soldiers soon discovered that they were not to be treated as equals. For most of the war blacks received lower wages than whites of the same rank. Unlike whites, blacks had few opportunities for advancement. When the regiments first formed it made some sense to assign them experienced white officers. But as the black troops earned combat experience, only a handful—fewer than a hundred—received commissions as officers, and none rose above the rank of captain. The Union's military commanders regularly robbed black regiments of an opportunity to demonstrate their bravery. Time and again they were given menial tasks as guards or work crews. White troops may have worn the same uniform, but they generally treated their new comrades with contempt.

When given the chance, black troops often performed heroically. During the Vicksburg campaign in the summer of 1863 black regiments fought valiantly at Port Hudson and at Milliken's Bend. Many Northerners were particularly interested in the exploits of the 54th Massachusetts, commanded by Colonel Robert Gould Shaw, son of a prominent abolitionist family. In July 1863 the 54th was given the honor of leading an assault on Fort Wagner at the entrance to Charleston harbor. In the carnage that ensued nearly half the regiment fell, including the famed young colonel. In an act of derision the Confederates buried Shaw in a mass grave with his black troops. His family replied that the appropriate resting place for a soldier was with his men on the field.

By the end of the war the Union's black troops from both the North and the South had provided ample proof of their courage under fire. Twenty-one black soldiers earned the Medal of Honor. Still, they never enjoyed equal treatment from their commanders. Roughly 6 percent of white soldiers died in combat as opposed to only 1.5 percent of blacks. In contrast, black soldiers were twice as likely to die of disease. Such figures are grim testimony to the fact that white regiments were more likely to be sent into battle whereas black troops often received unhealthy garrison duty with inadequate medical care.

When he imagined black military participation, Frederick Douglass envisioned a dramatically new future: "Once let the black man get upon his person the brass letters, U.S.; let him get an eagle on his button, and a musket on his shoulder and bullets in his pocket, and there is no power on earth which can deny that he has earned the right to citizenship." White reactions to the black volunteers continued to fall across a broad spectrum, but clearly their exploits helped moved white attitudes forward. Some whites echoed the sentiments of diarist George W. Fahnestock who wrote, "I only wish we had two hundred thousand [blacks] in our army to save the valuable lives of our white men." But others shared the modestly transforming experience of New Yorker Maria Lydig Daly when she first observed black troops marching through the city: "It was a very interesting and a very touching sight to see the first colored regiment from this city march down the street for the front.... Many old, respectable darkies stood at the street corners, men and women with tears in their eyes as if they saw the redemption of their race afar off but still the beginning of a better state of affairs for them. Though I am very little Negrophilish and would always prefer the commonest white that lives to a

Negro, still I could not but feel moved." At the very least
the sight of black troops drilling in camp or marching
through city streets became an object of intense interest. In
1863 Philadelphians flocked to Camp William Penn to
watch the new black volunteers as they had scrutinized the
first white recruits two years earlier. Some responded with
ridicule, but many were impressed with what they saw.
Certainly martial displays and tales of heroism did not recast
the thinking of hardened racists, but such information was
for some the thin end of the wedge.

The exploits of black soldiers forced Northerners to rethink
some of their assumptions about racial inferiority. Published
reports of black military heroism were particularly striking
when they involved recently freed slaves. If all blacks were
racially suspect, those raised in slavery were presumed to
have much further to go. Thus Northerners also watched
the contrabands' transition to freedom with interest.

The Union's military successes produced thousands of
freed slaves. In the first year alone ten thousand "contrabands" fled to the Union ranks; before the war had ended a
half-million slaves had won their freedom. President Lincoln had long doubted that blacks and whites could live
together in harmony. Before the war he had subscribed to
the popular idea that slaves should be freed and then sent off
to "colonize" distant lands, perhaps in West Africa. In
August 1862, as the number of contrabands grew, Lincoln
called five black leaders to the White House to discuss the
situation. But the meeting proved fruitless as his guests
refused to support a scheme to colonize part of Central
America.

Meanwhile, freedpeople's enclaves cropped up wherever
the Union army occupied Southern land. Often freed slaves
were crowded into disease-ridden camps supervised by the
military. Soon government officials and private organizations emerged to help the ex-slaves in their transition to

freedom. While offering the refugees much needed assistance, these reformers were also experimenting with the possible social and economic implications of freedom. Their efforts anticipated the much broader measures to come in postwar years. In the war's early years the freedpeople who had congregated on the South Carolina Sea Islands became the principal focus of Northern attention. Philanthropists journeyed to South Carolina to establish schools and provide medical aid while exploring the possibilities of land redistribution and social reform. And perhaps most intriguing to Northern observers, the freedpeople on the Sea Islands continued to grow cotton, demonstrating that their labor could be profitable without the force of the lash.

Northerners formed organizations to assist the Southern contrabands much as they created institutions to support the soldiers. Some groups, such as the New England Freedmen's Society and the National Freedmen's Relief Association, coordinated regional or national efforts. Others remained localized, raising money and sending agents south without a larger institutional affiliation. Like the two national soldiers' relief commissions, the various freedmen's aid societies ranged from religious missionary societies to militantly secular bodies.

Many of the volunteers who ventured south were young women who signed on as teachers. Esther Otis and three Oberlin classmates received commissions from the War Department to teach the contrabands. When the Union spurned her medical services, Dr. Esther Hill Hawks traveled with her husband to Florida and then to the Sea Islands as a teacher. There she found an eager audience. "The scholars love me and I love them," she confided to her diary.

Volunteers from the free black community found special significance in their activities. Several famed ex-slaves returned to the South to teach and provide medical aid to the freedpeople. Harriet Tubman visited the South Carolina coast only six months after the Union Army landed. Suzie

King Taylor escaped from slavery in 1862 and later returned to Port Royal as a teacher. Sojourner Truth traveled to Virginia as an agent of the National Freedmen's Relief Association. For blacks born in freedom, the experience of aiding the contrabands may have been even more powerful. Young Charlotte Forten, a member of one of Philadelphia's elite black families, put her abolitionist passions into practice by volunteering as a teacher in the Sea Islands with the Philadelphia Port Royal Relief Association. Soon after her arrival Forten reported her first impressions to radical abolitionist William Lloyd Garrison: "I wish some of those persons at the North who say the race is hopelessly and naturally inferior, could see the readiness with which these children, so long oppressed and deprived of every privilege, learn and understand." Although Forten came to love the children and adults on St. Helena's Island, many of her letters home stressed the strangeness of their religion and culture. Her time in South Carolina became an opportunity for learning as much as teaching.

At the outset of the Civil War there were 220,000 free blacks in the nonslaveholding states and thousands more in the border states that still permitted slavery. Although most Northern blacks worked in unskilled jobs, several cities maintained vibrant middle-class communities, with black lawyers, doctors, ministers, and shopkeepers. Isolated from white society, black communities supported a separate institutional world of churches, newspapers, and benevolent societies.

The North's black communities responded to the conflict's challenges as whites had. As soon as the Union permitted blacks into the army, leading members of the community stepped forward to encourage enlistment. In 1863 dozens of Philadelphia's black ministers, publishers, and business leaders signed an enormous eight-foot recruiting poster addressed to the city's "Men of Color." "A new era is open to us," they announced.

> For generations we have suffered under the horrors of slavery, outrage, and wrong; our manhood has been denied, our citizenship blotted out, our souls seared and burned, our spirits cowed and crushed, and the hopes of the future of our race involved in doubt and darkness. But now our relations to the white race are changed. Now, therefore, is our most precious moment. Let us rush to arms!

This was, they insisted, not only an opportunity to strike a blow against the Confederacy. By fighting, blacks could "Silence the Tongue of Calumny" and demonstrate that "we are not lower in the scale of humanity than Englishmen, Irishmen, White Americans, and other Races." Finally the authors reminded their audience of the heroism shown recently by ex-slaves at Port Hudson and Milliken's Bend. "Are freemen less brave than slaves?" they asked.

With black regiments at war, local citizens gathered to sew and prepare food to send to the camps. Black leaders also used their influence to dispute the pay discrimination and other humiliations the new troops faced. Northern blacks also threw themselves into supporting the various local, regional, and national organizations that assisted the freedpeople. In New York City a group of black women staged a gala ball to raise money for the contrabands. Ex-slave Elizabeth Keckley was a successful Washington dressmaker and confidante to Mary Todd Lincoln. As hungry refugees flowed into the capital, Keckley organized the Contraband Relief Association and began collecting subscriptions from blacks and whites throughout the North. Soon the organization expanded into the Freedmen and Soldiers' Relief Association of Washington, combining both philanthropic goals under one umbrella. Renowned author and runaway slave Harriet Jacobs dedicated herself to aiding refugees in Washington and northern Virginia by distributing food and clothing, nursing the sick, and opening schools for the young.

While Northern black communities became increasingly involved in supporting the war effort and aiding its victims, their status in white society remained largely unchanged. In 1860 Northern blacks lived in a world of legal restrictions and social segregation. In most states they could not serve on juries, testify against whites, or enter into interracial marriages. Only five New England states allowed black men full access to the vote. In New York black voters had to meet rigid property requirements. Elsewhere blacks, like all women, were denied the franchise. Most public institutions—hospitals, schools, prisons, cemeteries—either denied blacks access or shunted them off to separate, inferior corners. Only in New England were integrated schools common, though certainly not the rule. Blacks in search of public transportation, entertainment or religious worship faced varied circumstances: some communities granted them equal access while other cities restricted them to special "colored" seating if they were allowed in at all. Contemporary statistics point to a world that was both separate and distinctly unequal. Blacks fared worse than whites in health and life expectancy, literacy, wealth, and employment opportunities.

Not all Northerners were oblivious to the Civil War's ironic aspects. In 1861 abolitionist and women's rights leader Susan B. Anthony wrote, "While the cruel slave driver lacerates the black man's mortal body, we, of the North, flay the spirit." As the war became a conflict over slavery, and as reports of gallant black regiments filtered north, new voices rose demanding equal treatment for Northern free blacks. Some of the earliest gains came in Congress, where Massachusetts Senator Charles Sumner capitalized on the absence of Southern representatives to begin a crusade to dismantle federal segregation. In 1862 Congress approved compensated emancipation in the District of Columbia. Soon Congress

had banned slavery in the territories, removed federal restrictions on black mail carriers, allowed blacks to testify
in federal courts, and integrated the congressional galleries.

At the state and local levels, changes came more slowly,
but pressures for racial equality grew in the year following the Emancipation Proclamation. Cities with segregated
school systems faced protests from both blacks and whites.
Laws limiting black legal rights drew persistent fire. And
abolitionist whites, particularly in New England, acted to
reconcile their actions and rhetoric by desegregating church
pews, inviting black ministers to preach before mixed audiences, and slowly expanding access to institutions. Nevertheless, as the war finished its third year the gap between the
races in the North remained vast. It remained to be seen
how much real change in the North would accompany the
dramatic events in the South.

And even as emancipation and black military participation may have helped to open some minds, those same events
lay behind an upsurge of violence against free blacks. As
freedpeople drifted into the border states, whites repeatedly
voiced their anxiety over jobs and status with violence. Irish
immigrants in several cities grew notorious for their hostility
to those they viewed as economic and social interlopers.
After race rioting tore through Detroit, the *Christian Recorder*
reported that "Even here, in the city of Philadelphia, in
many places it is almost impossible for a respectable colored
person to walk the streets without being insulted by a set of
blackguards and cowards."

Most historians agree that ending slavery was the Civil
War's greatest legacy. The war's impact on race relations in
the North was far less dramatic but certainly important.
After January 1, 1863, the Civil War was no longer merely
about restoring the Union, it became also a war of emancipation. Many in the North resisted this transition, but its
general acceptance marked an important shift in popular

thought. The use of black troops also engendered significant controversy, but their battlefield performances forced many whites to rethink their most racist assumptions.

Black soldiers were just one group among many that played vital symbolic roles in this battle for equality and respect. The freedpeople in military camps and refugee communities became the objects of Northern scrutiny. Black volunteers who traveled south or worked with local benevolent bodies earned the respect of white co-workers and onlookers. Leaders in the black community accumulated precious political capital when they used their influence to support the war.

But while the seeds of a more favorable attitude toward black rights had been sown by late 1863, most of the benefits remained to be seen. This was, in many senses, still a story of broad continuities. Black soldiers faced unequal pay and unfair treatment even though the Union Army was more egalitarian than most of Northern society. At home, though reformers made some inroads in improving the status of blacks, their slow progress was a strong reminder of widespread resistance to racial equality. Even the changes that did occur reflect the war's tendency toward gradual adjustment. Abraham Lincoln did not turn to emancipation or black military participation out of a sense of moral righteousness. Whatever his private opinions, these measures were offered in the name of military necessity.

9

Politics in the Streets

THUS FAR we have emphasized the widespread support for the Civil War. But some Northerners did not share this enthusiasm. And others professed a willingness to support the war while still questioning the leadership of President Lincoln and the Republican party. Such dissent raises the question of the state of civil liberties in wartime. How did Abraham Lincoln interpret constitutional freedoms in a war fought to preserve that constitution? A second set of issues centers on political participation. How did different segments of society take part in the national discourse?

Through the long months of the secession crisis, many in the North favored conciliation with the South rather than military coercion. But the outbreak of war signaled a temporary end to open partisan disputes in most communities outside the border states. Even strong Democrats were outraged at what they saw as the Confederacy's aggression and were eager to see the Union properly defended. Southern sympathizers quickly discovered that their safety depended on hasty departure or judicious silence. Thus the implicit threat of violence—punctuated by the occasional fistfight—guaranteed universal public enthusiasm for the cause.

As the war progressed this early unanimity waned, and dissent began to emerge. Some strong supporters of the war chafed at the Union's inept military leadership, calling for their own favorites to be given larger commands. Others supported the war while breaking ranks with the administration over particular legislation. As the conflict continued, the catalog of controversial war measures grew—greenbacks, taxes, national banks, conscription, and, most important, emancipation. All attracted angry opposition. Where the administration countered dissent with arrests and martial law, new voices were heard bemoaning the demise of personal liberties.

This dissent took many different forms and appeared in various locations. The border states remained sites of ongoing tension and periodic violence. Old Democratic strongholds in Indiana, Illinois, and Ohio became havens for both open opposition and mysterious secret societies. Critics of abolition and conscription found especially receptive audiences in some urban immigrant enclaves. And just as for generations Northerners and Southerners had claimed the support of the Constitution, advocates on all sides insisted that their views properly reflected the intentions of the Founding Fathers.

The battle over civil liberties began soon after the firing on Fort Sumter. In selected areas, mostly in the border states, Lincoln suspended the privilege of the writ of habeas corpus which protected citizens from arrest without charge. Many prominent Marylanders, including the mayor of Baltimore, were thrown in jail during those first few weeks. In May 1861 military officials arrested wealthy Maryland secessionist John Merryman. When Merryman's lawyer petitioned the federal courts for relief, Supreme Court Chief Justice Roger Taney issued a writ of habeas corpus as the first step toward bringing the secessionist before a civil court. Military officials holding Merryman refused to hand him over, citing the suspension of habeas corpus. Taney, author of the controversial *Dred Scott* decision, responded by issuing his famous *ex parte Merryman* opinion, insisting that only Congress could suspend the writ. At this point the old adversaries were at loggerheads. Taney refused to yield on his constitutional interpretation; Lincoln continued to declare martial law by presidential proclamation, confident that history would approve his actions. In the aftermath, advocates on both sides unleashed a flurry of pamphlets arguing their constitutional case. For the remainder of the war the administration continued to suspend the writ of habeas corpus in selected locations, particularly in newly occupied territory.

In the fall of 1862, with the militia draft underway, Lincoln responded to a new wave of dissent by announcing that anyone guilty of discouraging enlistment or similar disloyalty would be arrested and tried by the military courts. In the war's heaviest spate of arrests, federal officials seized several hundred draft resisters, five newspaper editors, and a few political leaders. Once again most arrests occurred in the border states, but several Northeastern newspapers, including the *New York World* and the *Philadelphia Evening Journal,* faced temporary suspension for their critical views. By the end of the year the combination of military failure, controversial conscription, arbitrary arrests, and the preliminary Emancipation Proclamation had lured more and more Northerners into the "loyal opposition" camp. In the 1862 elections the Democrats gained thirty-four seats in Congress as well as the New York and New Jersey statehouses.

The next year the Copperheads found a perfect martyr in the person of Clement L. Vallandigham. Vallandigham, a Democratic congressman from Ohio, had been an outspoken critic of the Lincoln administration until he lost his seat in 1862. In 1863 Vallandigham rode the rising wave of opposition as a candidate for the Ohio governorship. Traveling across the state and the nation, the flamboyant Copperhead drew large crowds with his passionate attacks on emancipation, conscription, and the National Banking Act. But while other Democrats professed continued loyalty, Vallandigham seemed openly sympathetic to the Confederacy.

The Vallandigham problem came to a head that spring

when General Ambrose Burnside, head of the Department of the Ohio, issued a general order threatening treasonous dissenters with arrest. On May 1 Vallandigham challenged these regulations with a speech calling for the removal of Lincoln and suggesting that the Confederates be invited to a peace conference. A few days later Burnside ordered Vallandigham's arrest, and a military commission sentenced him to imprisonment for the duration. In Ohio the arrest made some sense. Open dissent by politicians and Copperhead editors had become a serious threat to the war effort. But Burnside's action put Lincoln in a difficult situation. The president could ill afford to renounce his general's actions, nor could he let the civilian Vallandigham languish in prison while his outraged followers turned his name into a rallying cry. The savvy Lincoln solved the riddle by commuting Vallandigham's sentence and ordering the Copperhead banished to the Confederacy. But Vallandigham remained a persistent annoyance when he escaped to Canada and campaigned for the Ohio governorship from exile.

As antiwar Democrats became increasingly open in their criticisms of the administration, uneasy Northerners shared rumors of shadowy secret societies intent on undermining the Union. Part fact and part outrageous fancy, these "dark lantern societies" were reputed to be working with Confederate agents who had infiltrated Northern society. The most notorious organization, the Knights of the Golden Circle, had formed as a Midwestern proslavery society in the 1850s. In 1862 the Knights attracted national attention when forty-seven of their members were arrested in Indiana. Another secret society, the Sons of Liberty, became embroiled in an elaborate conspiracy with Southern spies to free rebel prisoners in transit through Chicago. When this plan collapsed the frustrated Confederate operatives shifted their attention to an even more intricate plan to liberate prisoners from Chicago's Camp Douglas. This too proved an abject failure, resulting in a series of highly publicized arrests. The actual activities of the dark lantern societies may have been less important than their symbolic value to Republicans. Zealously patriotic Union Leagues were certainly more numerous and effective than their phantom adversaries. But by emphasizing the secret societies' treasonous plans, Republican strategists were able to tar all Copperheads with the sedition brush.

By the final months of 1863 the North had been transformed from a brief period of near unanimity to a world filled with open opposition. The combined weight of emancipation, conscription, arbitrary arrests, and expansive economic policy threatened to topple an embattled administration. How did the national authorities respond to this rising dissent? Certainly the suspension of the writ of habeas corpus and the suppression of Copperhead newspapers represented an expansion of federal powers. If the administration did not violate the Constitution, it certainly stretched it to the breaking point on occasion. As Lincoln argued, "Must I shoot a simple-minded boy who deserts, while I must not touch a hair of a wily agitator who induces him to desert?" Despite the troubling sacrifice of individual rights in a war fought to preserve the Constitution, perhaps more striking is the amount of open dissent permitted in the midst of a civil war. Although federal officials arrested thousands of citizens, only a small minority were incarcerated for their spoken or written words. And most of these "political" prisoners were freed upon signing a loyalty oath. One can make a strong case that Americans' personal liberties fared better during the Civil War than during either World Wars I or II.

Although the political cultures of the North and the South differed substantially, the historian Mark E. Neely, Jr., has argued that the two regions approached civil liberties more similarly than has commonly been supposed. Military authorities in the Union and the Confederacy arrested civilians at comparable rates, adjusted for sizes of population.

Both governments cracked down most enthusiastically in the border states. Jefferson Davis and Abraham Lincoln exhibited similar leniency toward celebrated opponents who threatened to become martyrs. In an interesting ironic twist, Neely suggests that freedom of the press may have fared better in the Confederacy than in the Union because Southern newspapers supported each other whereas in the North Republican editors either looked the other way or actively applauded when Democratic papers faced official harassment.

To place the official suppression of dissent in its proper context we must remember the power of *unofficial* suppression. In most regions Southern sympathizers had much more to fear from patriotic mobs than from overly aggressive police or military officers. When Clement Vallandigham traveled through the Northeast, local police fended off angry crowds wherever he spoke. But if violence—and the threat of violence—sometimes imposed an artificial unity on Northern communities, dissenters also took their case to the streets.

In the decades before the Civil War collective violence repeatedly disrupted the calm of Northern communities. Some riots reflected racial and ethnic hostilities, other episodes were more explicitly political, such as mob attacks on abolitionist leaders. The war years saw repeated episodes of collective violence that often combined a clear political agenda with traditional antipathies.

The worst violence accompanied the spread of conscription. The 1862 state militia drafts sparked a handful of violent incidents nationwide, contributing to Lincoln's decision to authorize political arrests. With the imposition of federal conscription the following summer, tensions rose. Communities that had easily filled earlier manpower demands now faced the prospect of a heavy draft. Workers chafed at the class-biased provisions which permitted commutation fees and substitutes. And with the Emancipation

Proclamation in effect, the Union Army had become an army of liberation, a cause for which many in the North had little sympathy.

In the months before each draft, federal enrolling officers reported encountering scattered violence as they ventured into hostile communities to identify eligible males. As the locally designated draft day approached, strains became apparent. Headlines urged citizens to meet the assigned quota, emphasizing dire consequences if they failed. Copperhead editorials assailed federal policies. Meanwhile, eligible men in saloons and fire stations brooded over the system's inequities and exchanged critical comments about the war's slow progress. It took little to ignite such a tinderbox.

The most notorious explosion happened in New York City in July 1863. In retrospect New York had all the ingredients for disaster: a powerful Democratic machine, a large free black population, and an even larger Irish population. The draft began without incident on Saturday July 11. But over that evening and the next day groups of disgruntled draftees, including a popular member of the heavily Irish Black Joke Fire Company, gathered and planned to disrupt the proceedings. Early Monday morning a crowd took to the streets. The four days of rioting that followed were the worst in the nation's history. Twenty thousand armed troops fresh from Gettysburg had to be diverted to New York to ensure order. By the time the ashes had cooled, more than a hundred people—mostly rioters—were dead.

The events in New York reveal much about the commingling of local and national concerns. In the riot's first stage the mob concentrated on draft offices and Republican newspapers and businesses, suggesting some combination of pragmatic and political concerns. But soon rioters—who were now mostly unskilled Irish workers—turned their wrath on New York's free black population. The Colored Orphan Asylum was burned to the ground; black victims were

lynched on lampposts. The death toll would have been much
higher had not most local blacks fled the city, leaving their
homes to the arsonists. Antebellum New York had had a
long history of racial violence. By mid-war those hostilities
had become intensified when Irish longshoremen battled
blacks for jobs. In the rubble of the New York City draft
riots we can find evidence of opposition to conscription and
emancipation; deep-seated class, race, and ethnic hostilities;
and rising concern over jobs.

New York's draft riots were the largest but certainly not
the North's only violent reaction to conscription. Across the
Union sixty local provost marshals were wounded performing their duties. In Boston troops fired on a mob that
attacked a federal armory. Several thousand protesters in
one immigrant Chicago neighborhood disrupted the draft
and then attacked the police who were called in to disperse
them. The violence was not limited to cities. Roughly a
thousand Irish quarry workers in Rutland, Vermont, battled
provost marshals and federal troops. Enrolling officers in
eastern Pennsylvania peppered the provost marshal general's
office with reports complaining of violent resistance from
the locals, particularly those in rural areas. When Irish
miners in eastern Pennsylvania's anthracite coal fields organized to fight for increased control over their workplace, the
mine operators claimed that the workers intended to resist
conscription. Federal authorities responded by sending troops
into the region to subdue potential draft resistance while also
crushing the upstart union. With this strategy the mine
operators deftly linked their own economic goals with the
military's fears of a disrupted draft.

Northern blacks were often victims of wartime violence.
In 1862 Irish stevedores in Cincinnati rioted against black
competitors, and striking New York City longshoremen
assaulted black scabs. Chicago experienced several outbreaks
of racial violence that summer. One episode followed a
black man's refusal to obey a bus driver's order to leave a

legally integrated bus. On another occasion white stevedores attacked a crew of blacks who had underbid them. In early 1863 Detroit residents were already agitated about the Emancipation Proclamation, the new Enrollment Act, and racial competition for jobs when a local black man was accused of raping two girls. An angry mob assaulted the jailhouse and then wandered the streets burning and pillaging until the military arrived.

Other episodes demonstrated the enduring power of ethnic hostilities. Chicago had a long history of conflict between German and Irish immigrants. The war's conflicts intensified these tensions as the Irish responded to emancipation by lining up with the Democrats while the wealthier Germans, perceiving less of an economic threat, were enthusiastically pro-Republican. On several occasions these disputes exploded in open violence. In Port Washington, Wisconsin, Luxembourgers—incensed at the 1862 militia draft—rioted against local German Protestant officials who had been accused of illegally manipulating the call-up. Sometimes armed violence took on a more specifically partisan cast. After Democrats converged on Indianapolis for an 1863 meeting, military officials confiscated fifteen hundred guns. On draft day in early 1864 several people died in Charleston, Illinois, as armed Copperheads attacked Republicans and furloughed soldiers to repay months of indignities. In the conquered border states, especially Missouri and Kentucky, roving bands battled in open guerrilla warfare. In some locations organized guerrilla companies and regular military forces engaged in an endless series of attacks and reprisals. But often even such guerrilla fighting seemed linked to antebellum hostilities.

Each case of Civil War violence can be viewed as a direct consequence of specific wartime tensions. Most can also be read as a natural continuation of antebellum conflicts. But neither interpretation fully recognizes the important process of adaptation that characterized the war years. Philadelphia's experience demonstrates how Northern adjustments to the war included shrewd efforts at keeping the peace.

In the decades before the war Philadelphia had a well-deserved reputation as an extraordinarily disorderly city. Irish Protestants battled Irish Catholics; striking workers attacked scabs; mobs assaulted abolitionists and free blacks; and members of ethnic fire companies regularly fought each other as buildings burned. During the war years Philadelphia had all the familiar preconditions for open violence: racial and ethnic tensions, rising inflation, a vocal Copperhead contingent. But despite angry debates over conscription and emancipation, numerous labor strikes, and even a visit by Clement Vallandigham, the city never erupted in serious rioting.

What explains this relative calm? Part of the reason is that Philadelphians were highly successful at avoiding burdensome drafts by virtually meeting assigned quotas. Recruiting was a continuous process of learning and adjustment, and Philadelphia learned its lessons quickly and well. The city also profited by holding its initial federal draft shortly after the New York riots. By the time draft day arrived, Philadelphia was an armed camp of police officers, provost marshals, and Union soldiers. This suggests a final reason why Philadelphians fared better than some other cities. In most of the major riots local police officers acted slowly or ineptly. Philadelphia's officials, in contrast, generally anticipated volatile moments and had the police out in force ahead of time. These preemptive measures may have been owing to the city's turbulent past. By 1860 Philadelphia had developed the nation's leading urban police force as a direct response to earlier disorders. Thus, in considering reactions to the war's challenges as a process of *adjustment,* it is worth noting that the conflict found Northern communities at different stages of development.

On the surface, the Confederate government nearly duplicated the national political structure. President Jefferson Davis's administration included a vice-president and a cabinet much like Abraham Lincoln's. The Southern states were represented in Richmond by two senators and congressmen apportioned by population. But some of the political conflicts that divided the Union cut even more deeply through the upstart Confederacy. Heavy manpower demands forced the South into draconian draft legislation, generating pockets of open hostility. Long months of inflation and food shortages tried the endurance of even the most loyal Confederates. Urban workers found their wages bought less and less. With so many men at the front, farm yields dropped. And meanwhile the Union's embargo threatened to strangle the rebel economy. In addition to controversial funding measures, the Confederate army occasionally impressed goods for military use. And for a brief time the government experimented with price controls to combat inflation.

While the strains of war pushed the Confederate government to act more aggressively at home than its Northern counterpart, Southern cultural traditions were more resistant to government interference. Where Northerners had become more familiar with the presence of taxes, courts, and public institutions in their daily lives, Southern society had remained deeply imbedded in a world of social hierarchy and deference. Politicians who had preached at the altar of states' rights and individual liberties were now expected to support a national military effort. Thus when Jefferson Davis declared martial law he faced even more emphatic denunciations than Lincoln. Some of his most vocal detractors were governors whose support he most needed. In the fall 1863 elections President Davis received a major rebuke from the voters: 41 of 106 new congressional representatives were openly antiadministration as were 12 of the 26 senators.

Some historians contend that the Confederacy's problems were enhanced by a failure of leadership. Jefferson Davis proved personally less effective than Abraham Lincoln. His cabinet was a mixed bag, with some strong administrators but numerous weak links and excessive turnover. Debates in Congress were more acrimonious than those in Washington, and their progress was hampered by inexperienced and inept legislators. Some historians believe that the South's best leaders chose to serve in uniform rather than as politicians. Another, complementary, interpretation emphasizes the absence of a two-party system in the Confederacy. Northern opposition coalesced in the Democratic party. Republicans battled Lincoln from both the right and the left, but the pull of partisanship enabled the president to maintain some control over unruly governors and representatives. Lacking any formal vehicle for dissent, Southern attacks on Davis became increasingly personal and destructive.

The Confederacy's worst home-front violence was concentrated in the Southern hills where companies of armed men battled the regular army and each other. Many of these guerrillas were among the great numbers of soldiers who had deserted from the Confederate army. Others were Unionists who had fought secession and gone underground with the advent of war. Most had become disaffected with the Confederacy's class-biased conscription legislation and the war's ongoing economic hardships. Even when these clashes involved political conflicts rather than purely economic survival, the backcountry guerrilla wars—like those in Missouri—often followed familiar battle lines. Antebellum adversaries used the cover of war to continue family feuds or revisit long-standing class antagonisms.

In mid-nineteenth-century America women had no formal political role and only a modest voice in political discourse. Women were rarely allowed to speak in public gatherings where men were present. In fact women's activities were largely restricted to the private sphere. With the coming of the Civil War, women in each region became more involved in private political discussions. Stories abound of patriotic women who urged the men around them to enlist or who bemoaned their own inability to fight. But did the war expand women's public political participation?

There is ample evidence of women venturing into public space to support the war effort. Women regularly attended patriotic parades and celebrations. Reports of a massive demonstration in New York's Union Square noted the presence of twenty thousand women and children. As we have seen, Northern women played central roles in wartime voluntarism. New York's Woman's Central Association of Relief was one of the war's pioneer benevolent organizations; the Sanitary Commission's Northwestern branch owed its success to Chicagoans Mary Livermore and Jane Hoge; and female volunteers were the lifeblood of nearly all local benevolent societies. But although these activities brought women into the public eye, they rarely challenged women's accepted sphere.

In some senses the coming of the Civil War stalled the progress of the women's rights movement. Since the Seneca Falls meeting in 1848 that heightened feminist consciousness, women's rights conventions had become an almost annual event. With the outbreak of hostilities, feminist leaders agreed to curtail their activities for the duration. Women's rights advocates nonetheless made important symbolic and organizational strides through the actions of the Woman's National Loyal League. Founded in May 1863 by longtime activists Susan B. Anthony and Elizabeth Cady Stanton, the Loyal League dedicated itself to petitioning Congress for legislation emancipating all slaves. Within a year the League's 5,000 members had collected 100,000 signatures, representing every state in the Union. By the time the states ratified the Thirteenth Amendment, the petitions numbered nearly 400,000 names, mostly of women.

Although the Woman's National Loyal League was ostensibly an abolitionist body, Anthony and Stanton also had a clear feminist agenda, insisting that women had a right to a stronger voice in political affairs. Their chosen strategy was not new; abolitionists, and women in particular, had often turned to petitions to publicize their cause. But the League's national structure and signal success set their actions apart from earlier efforts, perhaps paving the way for postwar organizing.

Other women challenged gender norms by delivering public lectures on the issues of the day. The Civil War's most spectacular female orator was the young Philadelphia Quaker, Anna Dickinson. Dickinson became a national sensation while still a teenager for her fiery lectures on women's rights and abolitionism. In the spring of 1863 she traveled throughout the North speaking to sell-out crowds on behalf of Republican candidates. The following January she spoke to a joint session of Congress with Abraham Lincoln in attendance. Wherever she traveled Anna Dickinson drew remarkable attention from the press and local citizens. Her detractors dubbed her "the wandering female Black Republican stump speakeress," but others hailed Dickinson as a "modern Joan of Arc."

Women in both regions also took part in violent protests in unaccustomed numbers. Confederate food riots were certainly a departure for Southern women. The rioters, including many wives of Confederate soldiers, adopted an unfamiliar strategy when they took to the streets demanding reduced food prices. Northern women faced fewer hardships and thus may have had less impetus to move into such unfamiliar political arenas. There were some episodes, however, in which Northern women also took to the streets. In July 1861 an impoverished group of soldiers' wives and mothers marched through New York City shouting "Bread, bread, bread" until the city council promised emergency relief. On several occasions women played critical roles in resisting the draft. In September 1862 a mob of Irish women stoned an enrolling officer in Luzerne County, Pennsylvania. This was followed by a series of similar incidents in neighboring counties, all involving women intent on keeping their husbands and sons off the enrollment lists. That November women in Ozaukee County, Wisconsin, joined in an attack on the draft commissioner. The following year a provost officer in Roundout, New York, reported that a band of Irish women kept him from performing his task. During the New York City draft riots roughly a tenth of those arrested were women, including many in their forties who may have had draft-age sons. This may understate their actual participation in the riot because the police probably concentrated on arresting the most apparently dangerous rioters.

The Civil War stretched the bounds of political discourse in all directions even while it left the shape of that discourse largely unchanged. Formal officeholding and decision-making remained in the hands of the privileged few, but more than ever before common Americans became caught up in the national political debate. Many remained enthusiastic about, or at least supportive of, the war effort. Others adopted various paths in declaring their dissent.

The men and women who spoke out risked arrest and public censure. Popular tolerance of dissent was one of the war's first victims; and while civil liberties may have survived, they were certainly bloodied by the experience. Many anonymous protesters voiced their disapproval with bricks, torches, and even bullets. Certainly some violence was motivated by economic hardship or traditional animosities rather than by political principle, but most episodes were fueled by hostility to particular policies.

It is possible to discern both strong continuities and new departures within this dissent. Certainly inflammatory partisan rhetoric was not new to American politics. Nor were urban riots against blacks or between immigrant groups. But the popular outcry against federal officials was, though not unprecedented, certainly new in its fervor and magnitude. And the increasing public role of women, though still unusual enough to be an odd curiosity, seemed to hint at wider participation to come.

The dissenters were engaged in a political dialogue with federal officials in which each side *learned* to play an evolving role as circumstances changed. If Lincoln and the Republicans had the military on their side, the Copperheads and the rioters had their own set of threats. Thus the president allowed strong-handed repression in the occupied territories but moved gingerly where flamboyant martyrs could do political damage. And even as city officials and military leaders learned to act aggressively in anticipation of urban violence, they recognized that there were other strategies to purchase calm. Following New York's draft riots, for instance, the city council voted to fund the commutation fees of local draftees through the sale of bonds. Some strategies were less benevolent. One Republican technique for keeping Midwestern Copperheads in check was to exaggerate the threat of murky secret societies bent on treason. And perhaps most ominous, the Pennsylvania coal operators who enticed the military into the region to help settle their labor problem were experimenting with a technique that employers would perfect in decades to come.

PART THREE

The Road to Victory
1864–1865

FROM THE First Battle of Bull Run in the summer of 1861, until the winter of 1863, Northerners engaged in a series of adjustments as they learned how to fight the Civil War. By the close of 1863 many of the Civil War's most crucial questions had been answered, its central puzzles solved. After nearly three years of bloodshed the North had learned how to wage war on an unprecedented scale. Along the way federal and local officials constructed institutions to direct war contracting, financing, and conscription. More important, Abraham Lincoln had issued his Emancipation Proclamation, permanently changing the shape of American life. And if many Northerners loudly protested, many others seemed to adjust their thinking.

With the benefit of hindsight we can see that the war was nearly over by that autumn. In the West the fall of Vicksburg assured the North control of the strategically vital Mississippi River. And in the East Lee's defeat at Gettysburg was the true "high-water mark of the Confederacy." But if victory true "high-water mark of the Confederacy." But if victory was already foreshadowed, the war's worst carnage was still to come. The final year and a half of struggle raised the question of the extent to which the Civil War had become a modern-style "total war." In addition to the war's heavy, impersonal slaughter and its strategic focus on civilian targets, the crucial characteristics of total war are heavy mobilization of the citizenry and increasingly centralized control. We must gauge how well the label fits the North's Civil War experience.

10

Total War in the North?

As WINTER FELL in 1863 federal gunboats roamed freely on the Mississippi River and Union forces under the command of General Ulysses S. Grant had secured control of Tennessee. But Lee's army, though crippled by its failed invasion of the North that summer, remained a major threat in the East. Before the spring campaigns began Lincoln elected to restructure the Union's military hierarchy. In March he appointed Grant to the newly re-created rank of lieutenant general—last held by George Washington—and named him general-in-chief of the Union armies. Henry Halleck became the Union chief of staff, charged with administrative and communications duties. Although Grant preferred to remain in the West, the president insisted that he direct operations from the Eastern theater. General William T. Sherman took over command of the Western armies while Grant established his base of operations with the Army of the Potomac, which remained under the command of General George Meade. Thus the North had established what one historian has called a "modern command structure."

This command restructuring elevated Grant and Sherman, who had each earned notable successes in the West, into positions of central importance. In the next year both commanders would help reshape the war's essential character. In the East Grant and Meade launched a ruthless assault against the Army of Northern Virginia. Calculating that Lee had neither the men nor materiel to match him casualty for casualty, Grant pounded away at his adversary on a series of bloody battlefields. Over seven weeks that May and June he suffered an astonishing 65,000 killed, wounded, and missing while the Confederates lost at least 35,000, with little prospect for reinforcements. By summer Grant had arrived at the strategically vital city of Petersburg. There both sides dug trenches and settled in for a long siege. In the meantime, Sherman led an army of war-hardened veterans into the heart of the Confederacy before stalling at the heavy fortifications around Atlanta.

Northerners watched these developments with chagrin. Even a people grown calloused by endless casualty lists found the Army of the Potomac's losses horrifying. Critics branded Grant a "butcher," and many wondered if a democracy could endure such tremendous costs. Finally, on September 1, Sherman took Atlanta, giving Lincoln new political life as the 1864 election approached. In November Sherman's men set off to the sea, destroying crops, farms, and the Confederate will as they went. By Christmas Sherman had reached Savannah and was prepared to head north to help subdue Lee.

Grant and Sherman's 1864 campaigns showed how dramatically warfare had changed over three years. Rather than fighting short engagements on isolated battlefields, Grant had his men in almost continuous contact with the enemy. Gallant open-field charges were replaced by remorseless trench warfare, anticipating the fighting in World War I a half-century later. As casualties mounted, soldiers went into battle expecting to die; some pinned their names and addresses to their uniforms so that their bodies would be properly identified. To the South Sherman fought no such battles. The Confederacy's Joe Johnston harassed Sherman's armies as best he could but generally avoided direct engagements. Instead Sherman's famed marches through the South became notorious for their assaults on the Confederate home front. Distinctions between soldiers and civilians seemed to blur as Sherman's veterans burned and pillaged with merciless efficiency. Here too the North seemed to be moving toward a strategy of total war, in which morale and resources, rather than armies and fortifications, were the ultimate targets.

In many senses the experiences of 1864 reflected lessons learned over the previous three years. The North's new command structure came after an endless series of experiments and frustrations. Not only had Lincoln learned, through trial and error, who was best to command his armies, but those key commanders had absorbed valuable lessons in the Western campaigns that prepared them for the strategic and logistical challenges to come. The soldiers had also learned their craft over time. Although raw conscripts continued to reinforce the Army of the Potomac, Sherman led seasoned veterans who had been in the field for three years and more. Finally, and perhaps most important, the Northern citizenry had learned—for better or worse—how to cope with the war's bloodshed. The losses that spring certainly strained patriotic enthusiasm, but a few years before they would have shattered the national psyche.

As Union fortunes ebbed and flowed on the battlefield, Abraham Lincoln continued his campaign to maintain political support at home. Time and again he sought to navigate his way between radical voices in his own party and Democrats who chafed at the war's duration and attacked Republican war measures. In 1863 Peace Democrats challenged Republican governors in a series of closely scrutinized state elections. Late that year an exiled Clement Vallandigham conducted a vigorous campaign for the Ohio governorship while Judge George Woodward ran for the Pennsylvania statehouse under the banner of negotiated peace. But the military successes that summer undercut the Copperheads' arguments, and outrages against blacks on the battlefields and in Northern cities seemed to diminish the power of racist rhetoric. In the end Republicans fared well in the 1863 elections, often with the assistance of absentee votes from soldiers at the front.

Meanwhile, Lincoln had to fight off threatened insurrection within his own party. Radical Republicans grew restive at the war's slow progress and mounting costs while questioning the president's moderate plans for Reconstruction. Treasury Secretary Chase, long a political thorn in Lincoln's side, assembled a core of backers and planned a run for office as the 1864 election approached. In February Lincoln confronted the secretary with his intrigue, prompting Chase to offer his resignation. As he had earlier, the president refused the offer, preferring to keep his irksome adversary close at hand. Finally that June, as talk of a Chase candidacy persisted, an exasperated Lincoln accepted his secretary's resignation. General Frémont led another abortive revolt in late May as Radical Republicans and a handful of Democrats met in Cleveland and formed the Radical Democratic party, promising racial equality, land redistribution, and the protection of civil liberties. The Radical Democrats never attracted much support, but the very idea of such a coalition is eloquent testimony to Lincoln's precarious position in the spring of 1864.

Despite these challenges Lincoln retained a firm hold on the nomination when Republicans convened in Baltimore that June. In an appeal to the War Democrats and Southern Unionists, the delegates called themselves the National Union party. The convention also dropped Maine's Hannibal Hamlin as vice-president on the ticket in exchange for Andrew Johnson, Tennessee's unionist military governor. The party's platform revealed how far the nation had come in four years of war. In addition to supporting the administration's policies and demanding "unconditional surrender" from the Confederacy, the platform endorsed a proposed constitutional amendment abolishing slavery. But in an effort to preserve party unity it made no mention of racial equality and completely skirted the complex and controversial debate over how to reconstruct the Union.

Lincoln may have secured his party's nomination, but he faced a difficult fight in the election. The enormous casualties in Virginia, followed by long months of stalemate, sapped the nation's enthusiasm for war and caused many Republicans to despair of winning the election. That summer the North learned that *New York Tribune* editor Horace Greeley, acting with Lincoln's grudging authorization, had conducted failed peace negotiations with supposed Confederate agents in Canada. The reports revealed that Lincoln had offered to discuss peace with the rebels, but only if they accepted emancipation and full restoration of the Union, terms that guaranteed fruitless discussions. War-weary Northerners took this as evidence that the president was willing to sacrifice thousands more Union lives in the name of abolition. Moderates in his party feared that Lincoln was demanding too much even as the Radicals urged him to support stronger Reconstruction measures. On August 23 a morose Lincoln had his cabinet members sign, without reading, a memo in which he declared: "This morning, as for some days past, it seems exceedingly probable that this Administration will not be re-elected. Then it will be my duty to so co-operate with the President elect, as to save the Union between the election and the inauguration; as he will have secured his election on such ground that he can not possibly save it afterwards."

Later that month the Democrats met in Chicago and nominated General George B. McClellan. The popular McClellan had long suffered the frustrations of a man convinced that he was better suited than his commander-in-chief to save the Union. More than two years earlier McClellan had handed Lincoln a memorandum at Harrison's Landing in which he laid out an assortment of political and military principles, warning against emancipation, confiscation of rebel property, and other radical measures. Since losing his command after Antietam, McClellan had become the hero of the Democrats and the party's logical challenger for the presidency. But before securing the nomination McClellan had to satisfy the party's Copperhead wing. From his powerful position on the platform committee, Clement Vallandigham pushed through a peace plank that seemed to go beyond the general's own belief in pursuing a military victory. In private negotiations McClellan convinced the Copperheads that, if elected, he would seek peace. To balance the ticket Democrats named Congressman George Pendleton, a Vallandigham ally from Ohio, as McClellan's running mate. The remainder of the platform spoke to all Democrats by attacking the government's military arrests and suppression of free speech, and calling for the preservation of states' rights, including—presumably—slavery. McClellan's carefully worded acceptance letter risked alienating the peace faction by declaring that he would insist on restoration of the Union as a condition of peace.

The 1864 presidential campaign turned the election into a referendum on the war effort and emancipation. Rival publication societies distributed a cascade of political pamphlets aimed at a wide range of audiences. McClellan's letter satisfied some War Democrats, but others bolted the party in favor of Lincoln. Radical Republicans had no choice but to support the president against a party that had denounced emancipation. Sherman's timely success in Atlanta, only days after McClellan's nomination, undercut all the grim rhetoric about military failure. Meanwhile, Republicans made political capital out of rumored conspiracies involving Copperhead secret societies and Confederate agents. Federal agents discovered intricate plots to liberate Confederate prisoners of war, stage election-day disturbances in several cities, and generally aid the rebels by disrupting life in the North. Most of these plans turned out to be more smoke than substance, but they enabled the Republicans to brand their opponents as traitors.

With the Union's military fortunes on the rise and dissident Republicans and War Democrats safely in the fold, Lincoln won the election with 55 percent of the vote, losing only in Delaware, Kentucky, and New Jersey. The Northern states gave the president roughly the same share of the vote as they had four years before, but this time he fared far better among Unionists in the border states. Republicans also received a major boost from soldiers, who were granted furloughs or allowed to vote with absentee ballots. Despite McClellan's popularity as a commander, in those districts where the military vote was separately tabulated Lincoln received an overwhelming 78 percent margin. In addition to their strong showing in the presidential election, Republican (and "Union") candidates won three-fourths of the seats in Congress as well as several key state elections.

The election of 1864 demonstrated the North's commitment to fighting the war to its completion. Racist rhetoric that had served the Democrats so well in 1862 failed to find receptive ears two years later. Had Atlanta held on for a few more months, perhaps Lincoln's forebodings would have come true. But now the Confederacy realized that its best hope for a favorable peace had vanished. Upon hearing the news of Lincoln's victory, Union soldiers cheered in celebration. For the rebels it was another blow to their already sagging morale.

Beyond its obvious significance to the outcome of the war, the election stands as remarkable testimony to the nation's devotion to democracy. In the midst of a bloody civil war the North never seriously contemplated delaying the vote. The election is also noteworthy in its adherence to the newly established party structure. Despite talk of splinter parties, such as Frémont's abortive Radical Democrats, when election day arrived the two parties coalesced into familiar competing camps with each appealing to the same demographic groups that had supported it in the antebellum years.

As Union generals pioneered strategies of modern warfare, the federal government continued to raise and supply an army of unprecedented size. By the spring of 1865 the Union Army numbered a million men. But changes on the battlefield did not necessarily stimulate parallel bureaucratic evolutions. The most important improvements in government contracting were already in place by the end of the war's first years. Private firms continued to bid for military contracts in 1865 as they had since Secretary of War Stanton and Quartermaster General Meigs first set up the contracting system. Federal taxation and banking laws had an increasingly important impact in the war's final year, but the vital legislation had been passed by mid-war.

If the booming Northern economy could accommodate the war's demands without major adjustments, the supply of manpower proved less elastic. Most young men who were likely to be swayed by patriotic rhetoric and economic inducements had already enlisted by 1864. On February 1 Lincoln issued a call for 500,000 men to be drafted the following month, prompting a mad scramble for recruits in most communities. When the three-year veterans returned home that summer, filled with stories of long marches and brutal battles, new volunteers became even more scarce. The government did all it could to encourage the veterans to stay in uniform. Those who "re-upped" earned thirty-day furloughs, four-hundred-dollar federal bounties, and unstinting public praise. But the Union stopped short of following the Confederacy in requiring reenlistment, and only about half the returning men elected to remain with their regiments. On July 18 the president called for an additional half-million men, with provision for a September draft to meet the assigned quotas. That December, with recruiting at a standstill but more fighting ahead, Lincoln made his fourth and final call, asking for yet another 300,000 men to meet February quotas.

Each new wave of demands put additional pressure on local recruiting efforts. City governments and volunteer organizations combined to offer progressively larger bounties. Some communities explored new funding measures by floating bonds or issuing special taxes to help fill local quotas. (In March 1865, as the war drew to a close, Massachusetts took recruiting out of local hands by establishing a statewide draft, the conscripts to be assigned so as to meet the quotas of individual towns.) But though these efforts became more aggressive with time, and bounties escalated to astonishing sums, the essential recruiting techniques remained unchanged from the first federal draft of July 1863. Meanwhile, Congress debated the merits of the commutation fee which allowed conscripts to pay their way out of military service. On the one hand the commutation fee kept a ceiling on substitution costs, ostensibly reducing conscription's class bias. On the other hand the provision generated revenues, not men. In February 1864 Congress ruled that commutation fees would henceforth protect conscripts for only one year. That July Congress removed the option entirely for all draftees except conscientious objectors. But though this legislation made it more difficult to avoid service, Northern men could still hire substitutes or claim any one of a long list of exemptions.

With the number of conscripts and bounty men on the rise, the Union had to erect more sophisticated apparatus to keep them in uniform. Desertion, which had been a problem for both armies, reached near epidemic proportions in the war's final year as men fled battlefields out of fear or in order to return home and collect more bounties under a different name. In response the army and the Provost Marshal's Bureau adopted more aggressive measures in guarding traveling troops and prosecuting—and occasionally executing—deserters, prompting some observers to question whether the new men were worth the expense.

One area of expanded government activity in both North and South was the maintenance of prisoner-of-war camps. During the war's first year commanders in the field worked out prisoner exchanges or paroles on an informal basis. In July 1862 the competing armies established a formal system in which prisoners were paroled on the condition they would not take up arms until they had been officially exchanged. This worked well and placed minimal strain on prison facilities until the North started using black troops. In May 1863 the Confederate Congress announced that the South would enslave or execute captured black soldiers and their officers. The North countered by stopping all prison exchanges and threatening retaliatory executions. For the next year and a half exchanges ended and prisoners of war languished in camps. Rumors of appalling conditions in Confederate camps, particularly Georgia's Andersonville Prison, raised Northern ire and provoked demands for retaliation.

Perhaps the most dramatic expansion in the power of the federal government did not begin until after the war when Northern forces moved into the South to help direct Reconstruction. But debates about the government's proper role in reconstructing the Union were underway by late 1863. These discussions had important implications for the future of the South and for the balance of power in postwar politics. Three crucial questions dominated. First, what should be done with the rebels? Should the vanquished be punished or welcomed back into the Union? What role should they have in their own political future? Second, how should the Confederate states be readmitted to the Union? What terms should be imposed? And third, what would become of the freedpeople? Beneath these questions lay another contentious topic: Who should decide such matters?

Abraham Lincoln's approach to Reconstruction followed from his principle that the Union was indissoluble. Thus, since the Southern states had never legally left the Union, their return should be swift and easy. He hoped to return the Confederate states to stable self-rule as smoothly as possible, rather than take the opportunity to punish the rebels or impose radical change on their world. In December 1863 Lincoln laid out his model for Reconstruction in his "Proclamation of Amnesty and Reconstruction." This plan promised amnesty and the return of all property, except slaves, to all but a handful of leading Confederate officials upon signing an oath of allegiance to the Constitution. The plan's second plank provided for the readmission of Southern states once 10 percent of antebellum voters had signed oaths of allegiance. Other than requiring that those receiving pardons accept the government's actions on slavery, Lincoln's proclamation was silent on civil rights for blacks.

Radical Republicans found Lincoln's "Ten Percent" plan far too lenient. Many saw an opportunity to reshape the Southern states; some called for aggressive action to enhance the status of blacks. After much debate, Congress countered with the Wade-Davis Bill in July 1864. According to this plan the Southern states would not be readmitted until a majority of voters had signed loyalty oaths. Moreover, only signers of an "ironclad" oath swearing to *continuous* loyalty to the Union would be allowed to participate in writing new state constitutions. Until those conditions had been met, the conquered states would remain under military rule. The Wade-Davis Bill went further than Lincoln in requiring emancipation (which Lincoln felt needed a constitutional amendment), but it did not yet mandate black suffrage. A divided Congress passed the Wade-Davis Bill near the end of its session, but Lincoln refused to sign it. Instead he issued a statement announcing his "pocket veto."

Reconstruction remained a divisive issue from the last year of the war through the first decade of peace and beyond. When the president issued his "Proclamation of Amnesty and Reconstruction" he was particularly interested in wooing the conquered Southern states back into the Union as painlessly as possible in order to make surrender appealing to the rest of the Confederacy. But in addition to expediency he also questioned the wisdom of the more draconian measures suggested by Congress. Lincoln's "Proclamation" also represented a crucial assertion of presidential power. Like the Emancipation Proclamation, it was offered as a wartime measure that did not require congressional ratification. The provisions of the Wade-Davis Bill, in contrast, almost guaranteed that the process of Reconstruction would linger long into peacetime.

The strongest evidence of federal expansion in the war's final year and a half could be found not in the Northern home front per se but in those conquered areas that had been returned to the Union by force. There civil liberties faced their heaviest attacks as military courts tried civilians for a host of war-related crimes, and there military authorities instituted temporary governments. As the war neared an end it remained an open question how long this newly expanded federal power would continue in place.

The North's private voluntaristic structure, like the government's recruiting and supply system, was largely in place by the war's second year. But as demands continued, the various philanthropic organizations cast around for new ways to finance their activities. Among the most successful, and certainly the most spectacular, were the series of sanitary fairs staged to raise funds for the United States Sanitary Commission. The first fair, held in Chicago in late 1863, raised more than $80,000 for the Sanitary Commission's Northwestern branch. By the end of the war nearly thirty cities and towns had staged similar fund-raisers. (Dozens of other community fairs raised money for hospitals or local organizations.) The largest of the sanitary fairs occurred in New York. Across three weeks in April 1864 the city's Metropolitan Fair raised more than a million dollars for the

Sanitary Commission. Two months later, as Union troops fell in record numbers in Virginia, a quarter-million citizens bought tickets to Philadelphia's Great Central Fair, which earned almost a million dollars. Overall the various fairs netted $4.4 million, with about $2.7 million (raised largely in New York and Philadelphia) going directly into the Sanitary Commission's general funds and the remainder to regional offices.

The sanitary fairs varied tremendously in size and duration, but they had many traits in common. The organizers raised money through ticket sales and by selling a wide array of donated items, including crafts, manufactured goods, military artifacts, and all manner of foods. Like London's Crystal Palace a decade before, they became occasions for celebrating American industry and creativity. The largest, including Philadelphia's and New York's, boasted widely renowned art galleries. These enormous fairs absorbed the energies of small armies of volunteers, organized in various topical committees and subcommittees.

At a time when Southern communities were struggling for survival, it is striking that so many Northern cities and towns could launch such ambitious spectacles. As fund-raisers they were highly successful. Perhaps as important, they gave citizens at home a focus for their energies at a time when enthusiasm for the war was running dry.

The fairs also complemented the Sanitary Commission's broader intellectual agenda. The USSC's national leadership had long emphasized order and efficiency in place of what they saw as the sloppy sentimentality of earlier philanthropies. In many ways the fairs applied these principles to local activity. Yet while the larger fairs worked through a sophisticated hierarchy of committees and subcommittees that suggested the war's new scale, antebellum traditions lay just beneath the surface. Abolitionist organizations had employed smaller fund-raising fairs for years. Although the sanitary fairs had thousands of volunteers, most of the preliminary work went on in small committees that functioned much like antebellum bodies. When volunteers joined committees, they followed the same associational ties—occupation, ethnicity, neighborhood—that had characterized prewar organizing. And the appearance of well-drilled units moving together with military precision sometimes proved to be little more than a thin veneer. As New York's Metropolitan Fair approached, an exasperated George Templeton Strong wrote, "All the committees are at swords' points. The quantity of gossip, intrigue, and personal pique that grows out of the Fair and its hundreds of committees is stupendous and terrible." The sanitary fairs also raise interesting questions about the evolving role of women in voluntary activities. Mary Livermore and Jane Hoge staged Chicago's fair with the help of several hundred women from across the Midwest. The larger fairs followed more traditional organizational forms, with male executive boards and hundreds of female volunteers. Such activities certainly earned these women widespread praise, but they did little to challenge traditional gender roles.

The proliferation of sanitary fairs in the Civil War's final year reflects the rising importance of scale and centralized control. Perhaps they might even be seen as a home-front counterpart to the emerging total war on the battlefield. But the fair organizers, and certainly their volunteers, never dispensed with traditional notions of benevolent organization. And while the largest fairs absorbed everyone's attention for a few months, the network of small groups dedicated to rolling bandages, visiting hospitals, or feeding passing troops plugged along without deferring to the Sanitary Commission's larger theories.

More than any other aspect of home-front life, the status of free blacks remained in flux during the final year of the Civil War. This should come as no surprise. Lincoln's Emancipation Proclamation, the recruiting of black regiments, and violent attacks on urban blacks had made 1863 a particularly tumultuous year for race relations, the repercussions of which would be felt for decades to come.

As black soldiers proved their mettle on the battlefield, new black regiments formed across the North. One of the war's most remarkable scenes occurred in April 1864 when crowds of New Yorkers lined Broadway to see the city's first black regiment march off to war. The irony of the moment was not lost on observers who remembered the black victims of draft rioting only nine months before. But while popular thought had certainly evolved, New York's transition was far from complete. The white regiment commonly assigned to escort departing troops through the city refused to partake in a ritual honoring black volunteers. And the antiblack *Metropolitan Record* marked the day with an article entitled "New York Disgraced."

While Northerners were growing used to black soldiers, anger in the South mounted. The Confederate government announced its intention to reenslave black soldiers and execute their white officers; individual soldiers and a few commanders threatened to kill captured black troops rather than taking prisoners. While the Confederacy (perhaps prompted by threats of Northern retaliation) never made good on its official threats, rebel troops did commit several well-publicized battlefield atrocities. On April 12, 1864, Confederate troops led by General Nathan Bedford Forrest (who would go on to become a founder of the Ku Klux Klan) overran a Union outpost at Fort Pillow, north of Memphis along the Mississippi. The rebel forces reportedly killed black Union troops after they had thrown down their arms in surrender. The Fort Pillow Massacre and similar outrages became a rallying cry for Union troops intent on vengeance. These episodes also joined New York's burned Colored Orphan Asylum as important symbols in the battle for civil rights.

The North's free blacks and their abolitionist allies continued to make slow progress across a wide front as the war wound down. On February 1, 1865, Bostonian John Rock became the first black lawyer to try a case before the Supreme Court. In Washington Congress continued to chip away at local and federal segregation. After Lincoln's second Inaugural Address in early 1865, Frederick Douglass tested the changed climate by attending the White House reception. When he first arrived Douglass was detained by the police; but Lincoln himself appeared and escorted the black leader into the East Room. Some Northern states and communities acted independently to dismantle their segregated systems. In 1865 Massachusetts passed the nation's first public accommodations bill, providing for equal access to theaters, restaurants, and similar institutions. Other states removed "black laws" limiting court testimony, immigration restrictions, and the like.

Some of the most interesting citywide battles occurred over the desegregation of streetcar lines. Many cities had already desegregated their lines, but individual companies in New York, Philadelphia, and Washington continued either to bar black riders or to insist that they only ride standing up on uncovered platforms. Such regulations became more awkward in the face of published reports of "respectable" black women who were not allowed to ride to visit their husbands in military camps and hospitals. New York's segregated lines caved in to public pressure in 1864 when the Union League Club announced plans to provide legal assistance to a mistreated black soldier's widow. The next year an aging Sojourner Truth discovered that legislative action was not always sufficient. Although Congress had banned streetcar discrimination in Washington, a conductor dislocated Truth's shoulder shoving her off his car. She responded by winning a lawsuit against the conductor, after which black riders in Washington generally received safe passage.

This impressive series of gains should not obscure the persistence of Northern segregation. Most changes were met with resistance. Efforts to expand the black vote beyond New England failed until after the war. The experience of Philadelphia's black streetcar riders suggests the tenacity of segregation. Despite many published stories of wounded black soldiers or soldiers' wives being refused seats on streetcars, most of the city's nineteen lines maintained their policies. Finally, several lines polled their riders, who voted in favor of continued segregation. Thus the battle to desegregate Philadelphia's streetcars continued into the postwar years and was won only with pressure from the state legislature.

As blacks struggled for improved rights at home, Congress continued to debate the future of slavery and the fate of the South's freed slaves. Although the Emancipation Proclamation had provided for the freeing of slaves as a military measure, many observers—including Abraham Lincoln—believed that full emancipation required a constitutional amendment. In the summer of 1864 the Senate passed the Thirteenth Amendment, banning slavery throughout the nation. At first the House Democrats, strengthened by their 1862 victories, managed to block its passage. But after the 1864 elections a handful of lame-duck Democrats succumbed to pressures, enabling the House to pass the amendment on January 31. Within three months most of the Northern states had ratified the emancipation amendment, as had the border states of Missouri, Maryland, and West Virginia and the three "reconstructed" states of Louisiana, Arkansas, and Tennessee. Only Delaware, New Jersey, and Kentucky voted it down. After the war the Southern states were required to ratify the amendment as a condition of reentry into the Union.

Before the Thirteenth Amendment was ratified most Northern states had already acted to end slavery. Maryland's voters barely passed a constitutional amendment abolishing slavery in the summer of 1864. Missouri followed suit the following January. Louisiana, Tennessee, and Arkansas also adopted constitutions ending slavery as part of their return to the Union. But enthusiasm for change was not universal. Maryland's amendment probably would not have passed without the soldiers' votes. The votes in the conquered states certainly did not reflect the beliefs of all citizens, or even the majority of voters. And although Delaware had only two thousand slaves, its voters refused to enact wartime legislation ending slavery.

With the number of free slaves in the South mounting and the prospect of universal emancipation becoming more real, Northerners grew more concerned with the transition from slavery to freedom. In 1863 the War Department created the Freedmen's Inquiry Commission to consider the issue. The federal government finally established the Freedmen's Bureau in March 1865. The bureau, under O. O. Howard, was both revolutionary and, from a modern perspective, surprisingly moderate. It was revolutionary in that for the first time in history the national government had assumed special responsibility for the welfare of a group of individuals. The bureau sent agents south to help the freedpeople (and some needy whites) with educational assistance, legal aid, and advice in achieving self-sufficiency. But in pursuing these unprecedented objectives the bureau had an extremely limited mandate at the start. It was established only for one year. Although agents could distribute abandoned land, they had no authority to confiscate property or otherwise provide ex-slaves with economic assistance. After the war the Freedmen's Bureau went far beyond its initial charge, but it nonetheless pursued a fairly conservative agenda. The postwar bureau established special courts and schools and adjudicated labor contracts. But often the agents seemed intent on maintaining social order and economic stability rather than helping to encourage the sort of revolutionary transitions that the Radical Republicans had envisioned.

In the final year and a half of fighting the Civil War changed more on the battlefield than it did at home. As the scale of fighting increased, the Union shifted its command structure and turned to new leaders who changed the war's essential nature. On the home front prisoners of war, armed guards on troop trains, and gala sanitary fairs reflected wartime evolutions, but the institutions established to support the war effort generally performed without major restructuring. Localism, voluntarism, and tradition continued to shape even the most innovative activities. The best evidence of expanded federal power was to be found in the conquered territories. There military governments maintained control while Freedmen's Bureau agents assisted freed slaves. Meanwhile, Congress and the president debated the nation's role in reconstructing the rest of the Confederacy.

11

Victory and Its Legacy

As WINTER ENDED in early 1865, Grant's men had laid siege to Petersburg and Sherman's troops were on the move north. Between the jaws of this vise stood Lee's 35,000 demoralized men. When the end finally arrived, it came quickly. On Sunday, April 2, the defenses around Petersburg crumbled. Lee sent word to Jefferson Davis recommending that Richmond be evacuated. Anxious citizens fled the Confederate capital as Grant's troops occupied Petersburg and moved on toward Richmond. A thankful Abraham Lincoln telegraphed to Grant: "Allow me to tender to you, and all with you, the nation's grateful thanks for this additional and magnificent success." On April 4 the president walked through the deserted streets of Richmond, accompanied only by a small armed escort.

News of Richmond's fall unleashed wild celebration throughout the North. New Yorker Maria Lydig Daly reported that "when I got the extra containing the great news, the tears rushed to my eyes, my heart to my throat." Washington marked the occasion with a nine-hundred-gun salute. Mary Livermore wrote that "the bells of Chicago clanged out the glad tidings." As soon as they heard the news Chicagoans rushed into the streets, lighting bonfires, firing cannons, and singing songs of celebration.

A few days later Grant sent a note inviting Lee to surrender and avoid further bloodshed. When a final rebel assault failed to break the Union line, the Virginian agreed to Grant's terms. On April 9, Palm Sunday, the two generals met at Appomattox Courthouse where Lee surrendered the Army of Northern Virginia. The magnanimous Grant allowed the Confederate officers to keep their sidearms, and any Southern soldier who claimed a horse or mule was permitted to take it home to tend his fields. Northerners responded to this latest news with another round of wild revelry, eclipsing the celebrations of a week before. Although there were still other Confederate armies in the field, Lee's surrender meant that the war had come to an end. In Washington enthusiastic crowds serenaded the president repeatedly throughout the day. In an emotional ceremony on the 12th, ex-Bowdoin professor of rhetoric Joshua Chamberlain, one of the Union's great citizen-soldiers, accepted the Confederate battle flags and then ordered his men to salute their vanquished adversaries.

The victory celebrations did not last long. On the morning of April 14 General Robert Anderson raised the Stars and Stripes over Fort Sumter, four years to the day after he ordered it lowered. That evening Abraham Lincoln attended a performance of *Our American Cousin* at Ford's Theater in Washington. Soon after the president arrived, John Wilkes Booth, a member of a famed acting family, shot Lincoln and then vaulted from the president's box onto the stage. Meanwhile, an accomplice was stabbing Secretary of State William Seward as he lay ill in bed. The following morning Abraham Lincoln was dead.

By the third Sunday in April, only two weeks after the fall of Richmond, the North was shrouded in mourning. Newspapers printed long, morose stories with black-edged columns. On Wednesday thousands of citizens filed through the Capitol rotunda where the body lay in state. Then, in a journey that was eerily reminiscent of his inauguration tour just over four years earlier, the president's coffin was boarded onto a train for its sad trip back to Springfield, Illinois. At each stop along the way crowds gathered to say goodbye to their fallen leader.

The dramatic month of April sent the North through a bewildering series of emotional highs and lows. Spontaneous responses to victory dwarfed earlier celebrations; public obsequies following the assassination went beyond any funeral rituals in the national memory. But although Northerners had never experienced such overwhelming displays, even these dramatic moments had familiar aspects. The victory celebrations were certainly grand, but their essential characteristics mirrored the rituals that followed other important battles. And the reactions to Lincoln's death followed patterns established with other fallen heroes. The North's rituals of victory and mourning had not changed much over four years of fighting.

By late May the final Confederate armies had surrendered and Union soldiers had begun to return home. On May 23 and 24 the victorious troops gathered in Washington for the final grand review. On the face of it this ritual symbolized a victory for the forces of union and order. But beneath the martial exterior lay an episode thick with ironic metaphors. Despite rhetoric about unity and reconciliation, white Northern men dominated the day. Although the shared uniform might have suggested discipline and solidarity, observers of the review remarked on the disorderly behavior in the ranks, especially among the Western regiments. Even the sense of shared victory was not entirely pure. Troops from the East and the West could barely conceal their hostility for each other. Thus the war ended rather as it began, with thousands of men coming together in a common cause but remaining highly individualistic and localistic.

Soon the veterans returned to their own communities, and Northerners joined in a final round of private and public rituals. Crowds gathered to meet returning trains; families welcomed home husbands, brothers, and fathers. Union soldiers who had lived through the horrors of war arrived home to a world that had suffered but also prospered. In the first months of peace the North endured the predictable dislocations of demobilization. As government demands came to a halt, some firms cut back production or closed their doors. Unemployment jumped just as soldiers were coming home in search of work. The returning men combined with the economic decline to stimulate a distressing rise in crime and disorder in some communities. But these problems were short-lived. What of the war's larger effect on Northern society? How much had that world changed over four years? What legacies did the conflict leave?

The antebellum federal bureaucracy was tiny by modern standards. A half-century after the Civil War, American intellectual Randolph Bourne, observing the effects of World War I, declared that "war is the health of the state." The federal officials who framed national policy during the Civil War worried little about such abstractions. Nevertheless, the pressures of the conflict did place new responsibilities in the hands of the state. How much did it accelerate the centralization of federal power?

As we have seen, several key pieces of wartime legislation took the government well beyond familiar practices. Conscription laws replaced state militia drafts with nationally orchestrated federal call-ups. Financial demands led Congress to approve new taxation, greenbacks, and a new national banking system. By suspending the writ of habeas corpus, the federal government selectively limited civil liberties in the name of the war effort. In the meantime, the Republican Congress passed important legislation on public lands, land-grant colleges, railroads, and a variety of other matters.

But the effects of these measures should not be overstated. The Union draft was more crucial as a spur to local recruiting than as a source of conscripts. The federal income tax took effect too late to raise much wartime revenue (and it did not survive long into the postwar years). And although Lincoln provoked partisan ire by suspending the writ of habeas corpus, most civilians who were tried by military courts would have been arrested under any wartime circumstances. Many of the crucial war measures were part of the Republicans' long-standing agenda for encouraging economic development. Thus this legislation may be best viewed as the political legacy of secession—and the resulting absence of Southern congressmen—rather than war-induced centralization.

Meanwhile, Northern citizens clung to their traditions of localism and individualism in the face of the war's centralizing pressures. Market forces, not the firm hand of government control, drove war contracting. Recruiting and bounty fund drives remained largely in local hands. Despite the nationalizing impulses of the Sanitary Commission and the Christian Commission, most wartime philanthropic activity followed traditional, decentralized practices. In short, if true "total war" includes the imposition of strong centralized controls on civilians, the Northern war effort fell far short of the mark. Although some intellectuals saw the war as an opportunity to impose order and discipline on an uncontrolled citizenry, most Northerners saw no reason to deviate from traditional values and practices.

While the Union was taking only modest steps toward expanded federal control, the Confederate government—despite resistance—adopted many of the same war measures months earlier. Confederate conscription laws were tougher and more intrusive than those in the North. And whereas the Union generally relied on private enterprise to supply its armies, the Confederacy—with very little antebellum manufacturing—employed a combination of government-run factories and independent firms. The South's most dramatic concession to the exigencies of war occurred in the conflict's final months when the Confederate Congress, after months of debate, approved the enlisting of black troops. A few companies of black recruits actually drilled in Richmond, though the war ended before they could see action. This astonishing turn of events notwithstanding, the South fell to defeat without fully mobilizing its resources. Or at least that was Jefferson Davis's view in March 1865 when he urged his recalcitrant Congress to enact "further and more energetic legislation" for raising men and impressing supplies.

With the end of the war, federal expenditures dropped dramatically and Congress set about retiring the war debt. For the remainder of the century, pensions to veterans and their dependents made up a rising proportion of the federal budget; in 1893 pension payments peaked at $165.3 million, or more than 40 percent of federal expenditures. These pensions, which went to 300,000 veterans and 220,000 dependents between 1861 and 1885, were one of the war's most important financial legacies. The conflict also left the federal government to administer the reconstruction of the Union. During the war the government had ruled with the heaviest hand in those occupied territories under military control. With the creation of the Freedmen's Bureau in the war's final months, Congress took a small but unprecedented step toward inserting the federal government into individual lives. Over the next decade the federal presence persisted in portions of the South. But even in this dramatic exercise of federal power Northerners could not agree on social or economic policy, and by the mid-1870s Southern whites had regained control in most states.

The historian Morton Keller has argued that at the state level, as nationally, governmental activism unleashed by the Civil War did not survive long into the postwar years before it was overwhelmed by forces of tradition and localism. Northern governors may have enjoyed their greatest powers during the war's first year as the Union turned to them to orchestrate recruiting. Soon, however, federal authorities began to deal directly with the citizens, circumventing the state houses. By the 1870s state legislators were intent on reducing taxes and budgets and curtailing their activities. As Keller noted, the thirty-seven new state constitutions written between 1864 and 1879 tended to diminish state authority in favor of local governments.

The Civil War certainly expanded the role of the federal government, but with peace its centralized powers quickly shrank. Still, precedents had been set. Income taxes, veterans' benefits, and Freedmen's Bureau agents all signaled a new relationship between the national government and individual citizens. Perhaps the war itself led those citizens to rethink their relationship to the Union. And with the 1868 ratification of the Fourteenth Amendment, which prohibited states from abridging the rights of "persons born or naturalized in the United States," national citizenship took on a special significance.

One of the ironies of history is that wars, while destructive, are often credited with spurring economic growth. The Civil War's economic impact has long been the object of particular scrutiny. The traditional argument was that the conflict launched the nation into remarkable late-nineteenth-century economic growth. One version of this interpretation stresses the economic stimulus provided by the military's demand for manufactured goods. A more subtle analysis emphasizes the war's legislative legacy and concludes that the conflict was a victory for industrial capitalism.

The argument that the Civil War created an economic "takeoff" presumes that the war somehow jolted economic growth out of its old trajectory. In fact, in the antebellum decades the North's economic output grew steadily while its manufacturing and transportation sectors developed at a rapid pace. As we have seen, available evidence suggests that although Northerners enjoyed prosperity during the war years, the pace of growth probably slowed in most sectors. Unlike in later wars, the military's materiel requirements did not demand major industrial growth. Most of the military purchases—food, clothing, animals—replaced civilian demands for the same goods.

National census data indicate that economic growth was relatively low during the Civil War decade compared with previous decades. Much of this decline was owing to the war's short-term impact on the Southern economy. The Confederacy bore the brunt of the war's destruction, both in destroyed crops and livestock and in the devastating loss of manpower. More important, the demise of slavery and the destruction of the plantation system had a dramatic impact on Southern agricultural output, leaving the regional economy in disarray in 1865. But both the war's destruction and emancipation were one-time rather than ongoing events. For the rest of the century Southern economic output grew as rapidly as that of the prosperous North, and after 1880 the South began making important advances in manufacturing. Thus long-term data suggest that the war neither crippled the Southern economy nor sparked the North into a dramatic industrial takeoff.

What of the Civil War's legislative legacy? During the war years the Republican Congress passed a long list of laws affecting economic development. Measures on national banking, currency, income taxes, and tariffs addressed the Union's need to fund the war. Other bills had no such war-related dimension. The Homestead Act opened up Western land to settlers; the Pacific Road Bill linked the East and West; the Morrill Act helped establish land-grant colleges. Collectively this legislation enacted the Republicans' agenda and in fact recalled Henry Clay's American System of earlier decades.

Although these laws had symbolic importance, their economic impact is less clear. The National Banking Act helped facilitate the sale of war bonds, but it did not necessarily promote investment and economic growth in the postwar years. Moreover, the nation's dual banking system—with both state and federal banks—survived through the century. The Union's fiscal policies left the nation with a greatly expanded money supply, but scholars disagree about the effects of the confused—and often contradictory—postwar currency policies on economic growth. The federal income tax survived less than a decade after the war. Some wartime tariffs helped Northern manufacturing, but their effects were partially offset by the Homestead Act, which drained cheap labor to the Western territories. Despite Congress's best intentions, land grants to transcontinental railroads largely lined the pockets of investors. The Civil War's greater economic legacy may have been in its impact on postwar leadership. For decades after the war Northern Republicans parlayed their wartime patriotism into electoral victories, producing officials who were sympathetic to emerging industrial capitalism. Meanwhile, Southern politicians campaigned on the "New South" gospel of railroad building and industrial development.

Although Northerners fought the Civil War to preserve the Union, they experienced it in separate communities, reflecting the persistent localism of nineteenth-century life. In towns and cities across the North, citizens shared many of the same small dramas. Civic rituals honored troops departing for camp and celebrated those who returned home safely. Newspapers faithfully followed the exploits of home-town regiments. Local histories tell of seemingly interchangeable recruiting tents, soldiers' aid societies, and bounty fund drives.

Beneath the commonalities there were also pronounced differences. Reactions to the Lincoln administration ranged from unfaltering enthusiasm in some New England towns to open hostility from Copperhead strongholds in the Midwest. Railroad hubs near the seat of war filled with disorderly soldiers on furlough or with wounded men recuperating in government hospitals; more remote towns saw only their own boys in uniform. Wartime rioting generally erupted in the most racially and ethnically diverse cities and towns. Although most of the North was spared the destruction that ravaged the South, some towns in Kentucky, Maryland, and Pennsylvania suffered destruction at the hands of invading rebel troops.

Larger cities may have been best equipped to cope with the war's challenges. For instance, Philadelphia's diverse economy and dense web of voluntary societies enabled it to adjust to the war's demands with minimal dislocation, and its large working-class population provided a ready supply of potential volunteers. Smaller towns responded well to the initial enthusiasm, but when the military called for new volunteers after all the likely men had enlisted, the towns were forced to look beyond their borders for recruits. The war also presented opportunities that could transform smaller communities. Springfield, Massachusetts, site of a United States armory, enjoyed a wartime boom. In 1860 the armory employed fewer than 200 workers; with the outbreak of war 2,600 employees jammed into the armory. The armory's output jumped from 800 rifles a month in 1861 to a peak of 26,000 per month in 1864. As the Springfield Armory prospered, the city of twenty thousand enjoyed a broader explosion in economic growth and civic pride. Chicago also grew rapidly during the 1860s, aided by the wartime economic advantages it enjoyed over its antebellum competitors, Cincinnati and St. Louis.

Some historians have noted the impact of the Civil War on local politics. In his analysis of politics in New York City, Iver Bernstein found that in the aftermath of the 1863 draft riots, Tammany Hall's Boss Tweed managed to ascend to power—over several other Democratic and Republican factions—by deftly manipulating the many political "possibilities" opened up by the war. Communities of all sizes had to contend with the war's mounting costs. In Massachusetts alone, cities and towns spent $13 million in public funds (and millions more in private donations) to finance bounties.

These expenditures sparked acrimonious debates about fiscal policies. Robin Einhorn has argued that the policy discussions surrounding the war's new expenses helped shift Chicago politics from a "segmented system" to "machine politics."

The Civil War was truly a national war fought by local communities. When soldiers marched off to defend the Union they were less interested in the abstractions of nationalism than in the concrete reality of their own homes and institutions. Citizens on the home front observed the war through the prism of local and state loyalties. But this very process of following the Union's progress brought Northerners together in a larger shared experience. In towns from Maine to Ohio, Northerners read accounts of the same military campaigns and viewed the same shocking battlefield photographs. Letters home from distant soldiers told distinctive tales, but they also had a common flavor. In this fashion the North's communities remained separate while growing together through common experience. This commingling of the local and the national culminated in the universal celebrations and grieving of April 1865.

Thousands of Northern women volunteered their energies in the scores of benevolent societies that emerged during the war. They rolled bandages, packed boxes, served coffee, and visited hospitals. To finance their efforts they staged theatricals, floral shows, fancy fairs, and various other fund-raisers. But while these actions earned widespread attention, most of the home-front volunteers worked within their accepted gender roles. Other wartime women, however, challenged these rigid barriers. Female nurses, who had previously been restricted to dabbing foreheads and dispensing kind words, began to earn professional recognition. Women traveled south as relief agents and teachers. African American women attracted public attention for their work with freedpeople in the North and in the Southern camps.

The economic roles of wartime women also combined largely traditional behavior with occasional excursions into new areas. Although the number of women in manufacturing grew dramatically during the war years, most of these new employees worked in familiar occupations in textiles or shoemaking. Others won jobs as teachers or government clerks, replacing men who had gone to the front. The absence of men also forced some women to take on new responsibilities in managing businesses, running farms, and providing for families. But their actions were really not very different from those of generations of antebellum widows.

We have also seen that Civil War women expanded their political roles during the conflict. At a purely private level it appears that women, like men, developed a broader interest in national affairs. Some also made unfamiliar ventures into the public arena. Women took part in everything from patriotic rallies to bloody street riots. Anna Dickinson and a handful of other young women attracted national attention by traveling across the Union as lecturers. The Woman's National Loyal League adopted a traditional strategy: collecting signatures calling for an emancipation amendment. Still, the scale of their operation was indeed pathbreaking. In addition to these more traditional home-front activities, a handful of women earned fame by spying for the Union or the Confederacy, and a few even dressed as men and went to war.

Immediately after the war several new books celebrated the "noble women of the North." Others credited the "Southern ladies" with keeping the Confederate cause alive when male hearts grew faint. Clearly the nation recognized the contributions made by women. Did this recognition translate into expanded postwar opportunities? Certainly these books carried no such implication. They generally praised patriotic women for performing their "natural" roles so vigorously. Narratives of female soldiers and spies sometimes took pains to point out that their subjects violated gender norms only out of patriotic necessity and only for the duration of the war.

What then was the war's legacy? As with later wars, many employment gains were lost when the men returned home. But after the war women did continue working as nurses, teachers, and clerks in increased numbers. The case for direct political change is weak. The founders of the Loyal League hoped to link the rights of women and blacks, but they were to be bitterly disappointed when the Fifteenth Amendment addressed only black suffrage. It was another half-century before women won the vote. Some historians have argued that Civil War activism taught women valuable lessons which they continued to use for the rest of the century. Members of New York's Women's Central Association of Relief, for instance, rejected traditional strategies for a more tightly disciplined bureaucratic approach. Lori Ginzberg has argued that this shift away from sentimental "moral suasion" was an important step in a transition from gender-based benevolence to a stronger class emphasis. Many of the women who went on to become involved in citywide charity organizing societies or other government-sponsored relief organizations began as Civil War volunteers. And some of the leaders of the postwar feminist movement developed their public skills in wartime organizing. Mary Livermore, who was instrumental in organizing the Northwestern branch of the Sanitary Commission, devoted her postwar energies to woman's suffrage and the Women's Christian Temperance Union. Thus, though the Civil War may not have led most women to question their position, wartime activism was central in forging the political consciousness of a crucial group of nineteenth-century women.

If the Civil War opened some doors for Northern women, how did it affect the lives of young men? This intriguing question produces more speculation than firm answers. When they enlisted, Civil War volunteers heard a barrage of rhetoric about manhood and masculinity. Recruits who marched off as youths came home as "men"—in their own minds and in the eyes of those who greeted them. Photographs of fuzzy-cheeked boys set beside pictures of cool-eyed veterans offer eloquent testimony that an important transition had indeed taken place. That transformation, which Reid Mitchell has called "hardening," could take a heavy toll before it was done, destroying many of the images that the young recruits took with them into battle.

At home, military service became synonymous with manhood. Eligible men who did not fight were branded cowards. Black soldiers who "proved" their manhood challenged fundamental notions of race. After the war the nation was left with a vision of manhood that embodied toughness and action, ideals that were not necessarily well suited to the economic transformations to come. Moreover, while thousands of veterans had survived the furnace of warfare, a new generation came of age with no such rite of passage, leading them to cast about for some way to live up to the standards set by their fathers.

By the close of the Civil War race relations in the North had undergone a major transformation. A war begun to restore the Union had become a battle for emancipation. Along the way 179,000 black men fought for the North. Even before Appomattox the federal government had acted to provide modest protection for Southern freedpeople, and Congress had started dismantling national segregation laws. In response to this swirl of events, Northern states and communities began to chip away at their own black codes. Abraham Lincoln's own attitudinal odyssey continued to his final days. In the war's first years Lincoln had resisted emancipation and rejected calls to arm blacks. By the end of the war Lincoln had moved much closer to the radical camps, privately suggesting that black soldiers and elites be granted the franchise.

The pressure for change continued into the postwar years. At the federal level congressional Republicans battled the new president Andrew Johnson over Reconstruction policies, including the rights of free blacks. In 1866 Congress passed a civil rights bill—guaranteeing blacks the rights of citizens— and extended the Freedmen's Bureau, both over Johnson's vetoes. That same year Congress passed the Fourteenth Amendment, which (among other things) protected the citizenship rights of native-born Americans. The amendment became law in 1868. Meanwhile, in a series of carefully watched referenda in late 1865, voters in Connecticut, Minnesota, and Wisconsin turned back bids to enfranchise black men. In 1868 Iowa and Minnesota finally approved black male suffrage, but eleven Northern states still denied blacks the vote. The following year both houses passed the Fifteenth Amendment, which forbade states to deny the right to vote on grounds of race, color, or previous condition of servitude. In 1870 the states ratified the amendment.

While Congress debated the fate of the Southern states, Northern cities and towns continued to remove discriminatory laws and debate desegregated schools. In 1866 and 1867 Rhode Island and Connecticut joined Massachusetts in banning public school segregation. Over the next decade Michigan, Minnesota, Iowa, and Kansas followed suit. Massachusetts Senator Charles Sumner introduced a sweeping Civil Rights Act in 1870. This bill, which prohibited discrimination in schools, juries, transportation, and public accommodations, was the longtime abolitionist's effort to throw the weight of the federal government behind desegregation. After years of resistance, Congress finally passed a modified version of the bill—excluding schools, juries, churches, and cemeteries—in 1875, the year after Sumner's death. But the nation remained uncommitted to such extensive federal powers: in 1883 the Supreme Court struck down most of the Civil Rights Act as unconstitutional.

The war helped create legislative gains for Northern

blacks and perhaps engendered attitudinal shifts among some whites. But too often in the decades to come the reality failed to live up to the rhetoric of racial equality, as legislatures and courts failed repeatedly to protect black civil rights. The war's greatest legacy to Northern race relations may not have come until the end of the century, when thousands of Southern blacks abandoned the South for Northern cities. In the South the pace of progress came to a halt soon after the war when whites gradually regained control of Southern statehouses. Reconstruction formally ended in 1877 when the final federal troops left the South, leaving blacks at the mercy of their former masters.

The Civil War's impact on class relations is less easy to gauge. Throughout the antebellum years differences in ethnicity, race, and skills kept Northern workers from joining together. For a brief moment during the secession crisis, organized laborers coalesced in calls for compromise. The outbreak of fighting brought all classes together in a surge of patriotism. But the continuing war—and the Emancipation Proclamation—soon drove workers into partisan camps. The strongest class arguments were mounted in opposition to the conscription laws, which clearly favored wealthier Northerners. Still, even the draft riots generally broke along ethnic and racial lines.

The war's economic effects cut in contradictory directions. The demand for contract workers and soldiers kept unemployment low. Bounties, soldiers' wages, and assistance to families of volunteers redistributed wealth toward the working classes. On the other hand, wartime inflation hit wage earners, particularly unskilled workers, the hardest. Heavy battlefield casualties left thousands of widows and orphans in need of aid. And although military pay raised incomes for some men, other volunteers accepted reduced wages, and many soldiers—and their families—suffered through long months of hardship awaiting delayed pay. Overall the war probably had only a modest effect on the distribution of wealth.

After the war organized labor continued to expand. New national unions pursued a broad political agenda, including demands for an eight-hour day. Employers too became more adept at defending their interests, sometimes borrowing the war's language of "stability versus rebellion" to further their cause. As they had during the war, public officials came to the aid of mine and railroad owners in their antiunion struggles, culminating in a series of bloody confrontations in the mid-1870s.

Throughout this book we have pointed to continuities in the North's wartime experience. The nation responded to the war's challenges with an ongoing series of "adjustments" but very few dramatic changes. The Union never adopted the wholesale mobilization of resources under federal control that we associate with total war. Why this stability? The North did not change more because it did not have to. Northerners did not go to war in search of change. They fought to restore the Union. They were willing to accept the war's various new measures—conscription, emancipation, political arrests—only insofar as they furthered the cause. And no further. Southerners, with far fewer men and resources at their disposal, were forced to accept far more dislocation as their price of war.

Focusing on *how* the North fought the Civil War, our emphasis has been on what individuals and institutions did. We should also ask how the war affected thoughts and ideas. Did the conflict change the nation's beliefs? Antebellum Northerners disagreed on a myriad of issues, but nearly all shared a set of fundamental values that had evolved from the republican ideology embraced by the founders. Republicans and Democrats alike followed the teachings of Jefferson and Madison in valuing liberty and civic virtue while warning against dangerous excesses of power. To these core tenets the nineteenth century added a celebration of equality and individualism and a deep commitment to democracy.

Northerners remained devoted to each of these values throughout the war. Meanwhile, they persisted in their faith in
tradition and localism while clinging to a world governed
by race, gender, and class hierarchies.

What of the values that drove the North into war?
Northerners said they fought in defense of the Union. As
the conflict progressed, the popular sense of that Union
grew from a vague abstraction to an almost tangible entity,
synonymous with the nation itself. The historian James
McPherson has pointed out that before the war the "United
States" was characteristically used as a plural noun (that is,
"the United States were..."). With the Civil War the
United States became a singular noun in common usage and
a single unified nation in the national imagination. McPherson
also notes that in Abraham Lincoln's first Inaugural Address
the new president used the word "Union" twenty times and
never referred to the "nation." In his brief Gettysburg
Address in late 1863 Lincoln demonstrated this transition by
using "nation" five times and never speaking of the "Union."
In the half-century after the war most new state constitutions explicitly acknowledged the preeminence of the national government, providing further evidence that the national
sense of self had in fact evolved.

In rallying to the cause Northerners frequently characterized themselves as defenders of law against rebel malefac-
tors. It was not just the Union and the Constitution but the
stability of Northern society that was at stake. Thus it was
particularly appropriate that citizens clung to their traditions
so tenaciously. In waging war Union soldiers, like many
warriors before and since, were convinced that they fought
with God on their side. Diarist George Templeton Strong
spoke for many Northerners in describing the sectional
conflict as a "religious war." Lincoln frequently yoked the
national cause and religious imagery, as when he comforted
a mother who had lost several sons by reminding her that
they had died on "the altar of freedom." As many Ameri-

cans turned to religion for comfort in response to the war, others melded their religious beliefs and political goals into a single ideology.

In the aftermath of the conflict the Civil War became an important part of the national memory. As images of the war's true horrors faded, Northerners celebrated its heroic aspects with songs, monuments, and sentimental fiction. Republican politicians learned to "wave the bloody shirt," rhetorically reminding voters of the Democrats' opposition to the war effort. In the South recollections of the "lost cause" promoted a distinct regional identity. Still, after Reconstruction crumbled Northerners and Southerners came together in a spirit of reconciliation, memorializing battlefield experiences while playing down ideological differences.

A final way to appraise the war's impact is to set aside broad national patterns and consider the experience of specific groups. Perhaps the war left most Northerners largely unchanged while leaving an indelible mark on a critical minority. For instance, if most women who volunteered to help the war effort never challenged their familiar gender roles, a crucial core of young women cut their radical teeth in wartime organizations. Similarly, a handful of Northern intellectuals embraced the war as an opportunity to further their hopes for a more organized, disciplined society. In the postwar years these men and women rose to prominence in the pursuit of scientific philanthropy.

The most intriguing group in this regard were the soldiers themselves. Men who marched off to war filled with high ideals and visions of honor returned to the home front with an entirely new understanding of themselves and of war. Many came home wounded; others were emotionally scarred or badly disillusioned. A few, like Ambrose Bierce or Albion Tourgee, put these painful experiences into writing. But many veterans came to celebrate their wartime experiences. Long after the war Oliver Wendell Holmes, Jr., who was wounded several times and once nearly died, wrote: "Through our great good fortune, in our youth our hearts were touched with fire." With time, more and more veterans came to share this vision of the war as a critical, constructive experience. Many ex-soldiers parlayed their military service into political officeholding as voters attached substantial weight to this credential.

For black soldiers the legacy of war was especially complex. Their battlefield performances earned them respect from citizens and soldiers, but many returned home only to face discrimination and abuse, particularly in the Southern and border states. On the other hand, black veterans often rose to positions of prominence within black communities. According to Joseph Glatthaar, white officers who commanded black troops faced a particularly difficult transition after the war. A disproportionate number divorced, fell into alcoholism, or committed suicide, perhaps suggesting that their wartime status as pariahs robbed them of the emotional comfort that other veterans enjoyed.

In 1866 a group of veterans established the Grand Army of the Republic. For the rest of the century the GAR served as a political organization, a fraternal society, and a powerful lobbying force. By the 1890s the veterans' group had become invested in establishing its own glorious version of the Civil War as the nation's official narrative. In these veterans' carefully constructed memory, military life was disciplined, heroic, and strenuous. And, most important, the Union veterans claimed responsibility for preserving the nation against a cataclysmic threat. What they failed to recognize was that in the decades following the Civil War the world they had fought to preserve had evolved into a very different place.

A Note on Sources

GENERAL AND LOCAL HISTORIES

Anyone wishing to understand the Civil War era should begin with James M. McPherson's *Battle Cry of Freedom: The Civil War Era* (New York, 1988) and *Ordeal by Fire: The Civil War and Reconstruction* (2nd ed., New York, 1992). But readers should not neglect Allan Nevins's superb four-volume *The War for the Union* (New York, 1959–1971). The revised edition of *Ordeal by Fire* has an excellent detailed bibliography, but for more bibliographic information see Eugene C. Murdock, *The Civil War in the North: A Selective Annotated Bibliography* (New York, 1987). Garold L. Cole, *Civil War Eyewitnesses: An Annotated Bibliography of Books and Articles, 1955–1986* (Columbia, S.C., 1986), is a comprehensive, well-indexed list of published accounts by soldiers and civilians. Eugene B. Long, *The Civil War Day by Day: An Almanac, 1861–1865* (Garden City, N.Y., 1971) is an invaluable reference.

On the North see Phillip Shaw Paludan, *"A People's Contest": The Union and Civil War, 1861–1865* (New York, 1989), which also includes an excellent bibliographic essay. Although now superseded by Paludan, Emerson David Fite, *Social and Economic Conditions in the North* (New York, 1910) is still valuable for information on the home front. For a useful collection of primary sources see Charles Winston Smith and Charles Judah, eds., *Life in the North During the Civil War: A Source History* (Albuquerque, N.M., 1966). And for a sampling of recent scholarship see Maris Vinovskis, ed., *Toward a Social History of the American Civil War: Exploratory Essays* (New York, 1990). Vinovskis's "Have Social Historians Lost the Civil War? Some Preliminary Demographic Speculations," reprinted in his collection, is a good introduction to the demographic issues. Two general histories of the Confederacy are Clement

Eaton, *A History of the Southern Confederacy* (New York, 1954), and Emory Thomas, *The Confederate Nation, 1861–1865* (New York, 1979).

Many of the arguments in this book appeared in an earlier form in J. Matthew Gallman, *Mastering Wartime: A Social History of Philadelphia During the Civil War* (New York, 1990). See the notes to that book for a fuller coverage of scholarly articles. Iver Bernstein, *The New York City Draft Riots: Their Significance for American Society and Politics in the Age of the Civil War* (New York, 1990) emphasizes political developments in that city. For a broader history see Earnest A. McKay, *The Civil War and New York City* (Syracuse, 1990). Theodore J. Karamanski, *Rally 'Round the Flag: Chicago and the Civil War* (Chicago, 1993) is a useful narrative but should be supplemented with Robin Einhorn's "The Civil War and Municipal Government in Chicago," in the Maris Vinovskis collection. Thomas R. Kemp's "Community and War: The Civil War Experience in Two New Hampshire Towns," also in the Vinovskis collection, examines Claremont and Newport, New Hampshire. For an account of one Massachusetts town see Emily J. Harris, "Sons and Soldiers: Deerfield, Massachusetts, and the Civil War," *Civil War History* 30 (June 1984), 157–171. Most nineteenth-century Northern community studies pay scant attention to the Civil War's impact. Two excellent exceptions are: Michael Frisch, *Town into City: Springfield, Massachusetts, and the Meaning of Community, 1840–1880* (Cambridge, Mass., 1972), and Don Harrison Doyle, *The Social Order of a Frontier Community: Jacksonville, Illinois, 1825–70* (Urbana, 1978).

Specific Topics

T. Harry Williams, *Lincoln and His Generals* (New York, 1952) remains an excellent account of the North's military adjustments to war. For a general history of Northern politics see James A. Rawley, *The Politics of Union: Northern Politics During the Civil War* (Lincoln, Nebr., 1974). For a fascinating insider's account by Lincoln's private secretary see Tyler

Dennett, ed., *Lincoln and the Civil War in the Diaries and Letters of John Hay* (1939; New York, 1988). The Democratic party is examined in Joel Silbey, *A Respectable Minority: The Democratic Party in the Civil War Era* (New York, 1977). On Congress's role, see Allan G. Bogue, *The Congressman's Civil War* (New York, 1989). For the intersection of labor and politics see David Montgomery, *Beyond Equality: Labor and the Radical Republicans, 1862–1872* (New York, 1967). Eric L. McKitrick's "Party Politics and the Union and Confederate War Efforts," in William Nesbet Chambers and Walter Dean Burnham, eds., *The American Party Systems* (New York, 1967), is an excellent comparison of the two political systems. For a provocative comparative analysis of wartime legislation in the North and South see Richard F. Bensel, *Yankee Leviathan: The Origins of Central State Authority in America, 1859–1877* (New York, 1990).

We still have no full analysis of the war's impact on Northern women. Two useful surveys are Agatha Young, *Women and the Crisis: Women of the North in the Civil War* (New York, 1959), and Mary Elizabeth Massey, *Bonnet Brigades* (New York, 1966) (which also discusses the South). Three recent books discuss important aspects of women's public activism: Mary Ryan, *Women in Public: Between Banners and Ballots, 1825–1880* (Baltimore, 1990); Lori D. Ginzberg, *Women and the Work of Benevolence: Morality, Politics, and Class in the 19th-Century United States* (New Haven, 1990); and Wendy Hamand Venet, *Neither Ballots nor Bullets: Women Abolitionists and the Civil War* (Charlottesville, Va., 1991). Marilyn Mayer Culpepper's *Trials and Triumphs: The Women of the American Civil War* (East Lansing, Mich., 1991) is an excellent collection of primary sources on the experiences of white women. On the experiences of black women see Dorothy Sterling, ed., *We Are Your Sisters: Black Women in the Nineteenth Century* (New York, 1984). For recent literature on gender in both the North and the South see Catherine Clinton and Nina Silber, eds., *Divided Houses: Gender and the Civil War* (New York, 1992). George C. Rable, *Civil Wars: Women and the Crisis of Southern Nationalism* (Urbana, 1991) surveys the history of Confederate women.

On the North's manpower adjustments see James W. Geary, *We Need Men: The Union Draft in the Civil War* (DeKalb, Ill., 1991), and Eugene C. Murdock, *One Million Men: The Civil War Draft in the North* (Madison, Wisc., 1971). Geary examines the extensive article literature on this topic, but see also his "Civil War Conscription in the North: A Historiographical Review," *Civil War History* 32 (September 1986), 208–228, and Gallman, *Mastering Wartime.*

There is no full study of the effects of wartime separation and death, but Culpepper, ed., *Trials and Triumphs* contains a wealth of useful documents. Several recent books have explored the experiences of Civil War soldiers: see Reid Mitchell, *Civil War Soldiers: Their Expectations and Their Experiences* (New York, 1988); Mitchell, *The Vacant Chair: The Northern Soldier Leaves Home* (New York, 1993); and Gerald Linderman, *Embattled Courage: The Experience of Combat in the American Civil War* (New York, 1987). Three studies of Northern thought and culture are: Earl J. Hess, *Liberty, Virtue, and Progress: Northerners and Their War for the Union* (New York, 1988); Randall C. Jimerson, *The Private Civil War: Popular Thought During the Sectional Conflict* (Baton Rouge, 1988); and Anne C. Rose, *Victorian America and the Civil War* (New York, 1992). On religion see James Moorhead, *American Apocalypse: Yankee Protestants in the Civil War, 1860–1869* (New Haven, 1978). George M. Fredrickson, *The Inner Civil War: Northern Intellectuals and the Crisis of the Union* (New York, 1965) explores the war's impact on Northern thinkers; Daniel Aaron, *The Unwritten War: American Writers and the Civil War* (New York, 1973) examines authors' reactions to the conflict. Louis P. Masur considers fourteen wartime authors in *The Real War Will Never Get into the Books: Selections from Writers During the Civil War* (New York, 1993). For a catalog of Civil War fiction written both during and after the war see Albert J. Menendez, *Civil War Novels: An Annotated Bibliography* (New York, 1986).

Many of the crucial articles and statistics on the economic impact of the Civil War are collected in David Gilchrist and W. David Lewis, eds., *Economic Change in the Civil War Era* (Greenville, Del., 1965), and Ralph Andreano, ed., *The Economic Impact of the Civil War* (2nd ed., Cambridge, Mass.,

1967). But see also Stanley L. Engerman, "The Economic Impact of the Civil War," *Explorations in Entrepreneurial History* 3 (Spring/Summer 1966), 176–199. Claudia D. Goldin and Frank D. Lewis, "The Economic Costs of the American Civil War: Estimates and Implications," *Journal of Economic History* 35 (June 1975), 299–325, estimates the war's direct and indirect costs. Patrick O'Brien, *The Economic Effects of the American Civil War* (London, 1988), and Roger Ransom, *Conflict and Compromise: The Political Economy of Slavery, Emancipation, and the American Civil War* (New York, 1989) bring the debate up to date. Grace Palladino, *Another Civil War: Labor, Capital, and the State in the Anthracite Regions of Pennsylvania, 1840–68* (Urbana, 1990) discusses the war's impact on class relations in a mining district.

Civil War benevolence is surveyed in Robert H. Bremner, *The Public Good: Philanthropy and Welfare in the Civil War Era* (New York, 1980). For the history of the United States Sanitary Commission see William Q. Maxwell, *Lincoln's Fifth Wheel: The Political History of the United States Sanitary Commission* (New York, 1956); but also see Fredrickson's *The Inner Civil War*. Several of the books on women, cited above, emphasize benevolent work. Many of the leading patriotic pamphlets are assembled in Frank Freidel, ed., *Union Pamphlets of the Civil War, 1861–1865* (2 vols., Cambridge, Mass., 1967).

The best account of emancipation and its aftermath is James M. McPherson, *The Struggle for Equality* (Princeton, N.J., 1964). A wealth of primary materials on the black wartime experience are assembled in Ira Berlin, et al, eds., *Freedom: A Documentary History of Emancipation*. In particular see Series II, *The Black Military Experience* (Cambridge, Mass., 1985). McPherson's *The Negro's Civil War* (New York, 1965) is another valuable collection. On the experiences of black women see Sterling, ed., *We Are Your Sisters*. And for the relationship between black soldiers and white officers consult Joseph Glatthaar, *Forged in Battle: The Civil War Alliance of Black Soldiers and White Officers* (New York, 1990).

For a fascinating account of the war's numerous constitutional issues see Mark E. Neely, Jr., *The Fate of Liberty: Abraham Lincoln and Civil Liberties* (New York, 1991). Neely compares the North and the South in a published lecture, *Confederate Bastille: Jefferson Davis and Civil Liberties* (Milwaukee, 1993), and in a forthcoming book on the same topic. The nation's worst wartime rioting is the subject of Adrian Cook, *The Armies of the Streets: The New York City Draft Riots of 1863* (Lexington, Ky., 1974), and Bernstein's *The New York City Draft Riots*. Palladino's *The Other Civil War* discusses disruptions in Pennsylvania's coal counties; Geary's *We Need Men* has numerous descriptions of antidraft violence. The extensive article literature on wartime rioting is summarized in Gallman, "Preserving the Peace: Order and Disorder in Civil War Philadelphia," *Pennsylvania History* 55 (October 1988), 201–215. For an account of border state violence, see Michael Fellman, *Inside War: The Guerrilla Conflict in Missouri During the American Civil War* (New York, 1989). Phillip Shaw Paludan's *Victims: A True History of the Civil War* (Knoxville, Tenn., 1981) is a gripping account of guerrilla warfare in the hills of North Carolina.

The issue of total war is discussed in Mark Neely, "Was the Civil War a Total War?" *Civil War History* 37 (March 1991), 5–28. For a collection of essays which address the question from various angles, see Joerg Nagler and Stig Förster, eds., *On the Road to Total War: The American Civil War and the German Wars of Unification, 1861–1871* (forthcoming). Morton Keller's *Affairs of State: Public Life in Late Nineteenth Century America* (Cambridge, Mass., 1977) analyzes the war's effect on postwar America. For an excellent account of Reconstruction, including a discussion of the wartime debates, see Eric Foner, *Reconstruction: America's Unfinished Revolution, 1863–1877* (New York, 1988). And for the postwar experience of Union veterans see Stuart McConnell, *Glorious Contentment: The Grand Army of the Republic, 1865–1900* (Chapel Hill, 1992).

Index

Aaron, Daniel, 87, 88
Adams, Henry, 87
African Americans. *See* Blacks.
Agriculture, 25, 102
Alcott, Louisa May, 86
American Anti-Slavery Society,
   110, 122
American Temperance Union, 90
Anderson, Robert, 11–12, 179
Andersonville Prison, 168
Anglo-African (New York), 131
Anthony, Susan B., 138, 153
Antietam, battle of, 41, 128
Appomattox Courthouse, 179
Arkansas, 9, 12, 175
Armour, Philip, 103
Army, Union: antebellum, 31–32;
   organization and command
   structure, 15, 58–60, 159–160;
   representativeness, 66–68. *See
   also* Enlistment and recruiting.
Arrests, political, 142–144
Ashhurst, Richard, 80
Atlanta, 160

Baker, E. D., 11
Baltimore, 20, 162; riots, 13–14
Banking, 20, 26, 96, 166, 181,
   185–186. *See also* National
   Banking Act.
Barnum, P. T., 84
Barton, Clara, 124
Battle Pieces (Melville), 88
Bellows, Henry W., 110–111
Belmont, August, 119
Bernstein, Iver, 187
Bierce, Ambrose, 88, 196

Black soldiers, 17, 75, 129–134,
   197; in the Confederacy,
   182–183; and masculinity, 191;
   and prisoners of war, 168;
   responses to, 173
Blacks, 17, 23, 28; and
   Reconstruction, 169–170; status
   of, 138–139, 172–177, 191–194;
   victims of violence, 147–148;
   and voluntarism, 113, 135–136;
   and war effort, 136–137; white
   attitudes toward, 133–134. *See
   also* Black soldiers;
   Emancipation; individual
   names.
Blackwell, Emily, 118
Booth, Edwin, 84
Booth, John Wilkes, 179
Boston, 148
Bounties, 64–65, 167
Bourne, Randolph, 181
Bragg, Braxton, 42
Breckenridge, John C., 6
Brown, William Wells, 131
Buchanan, James, 5, 8, 11
Buell, Don Carlos, 42
Bull Run: first battle of, 21, 40,
   46; second battle of, 41
Burnside, Ambrose, 42, 144
Butler, Benjamin, 126

Cameron, Simon, 19, 60
Carnegie, Andrew, 103
Casualties, war, 74–75
Chamberlain, Joshua, 179
Chambersburg, Pa., 113
Chancellorsville, battle of, 42

Chapin, Sarah, 80, 83
Charleston, Ill., 149
Charleston Mercury, 13
Chase, Salmon P., 19, 20, 45, 46,
    50–51, 95–97, 162
Chicago, 65, 90, 113, 114, 144,
    148, 170, 178, 188; economy,
    102–103, 187; violence in,
    148–149
Christian Recorder (Philadelphia),
    131, 139
Cincinnati, 148
Civil liberties, 20, 48, 141–146,
    170, 181–182. *See also* Habeas
    corpus.
Colleges and universities, 88
Collis, Septima, 83
Communities, 15, 186–188
Commutation, 64, 71, 167
Confederacy, 8, 12; and black
    Union troops, 173; casualties,
    75; centralization in, 182–183;
    civil liberties in, 145–146;
    conscription in, 66, 72–73;
    economy, 101, 108, 185;
    enlistment and recruiting in,
    166; finance, 95, 98–99;
    military skills, 32; politics in,
    54–55, 151–152; population,
    22–23; and secession, 8–13;
    Southern women, 82, 106;
    supply system, 94; violence in,
    152, 154
Congress, 37th, 45–48, 51–52
Connecticut, 61, 192
Conscription, 20, 60–73, 166–167,
    181; in the Confederacy, 66,
    72–73; evaluation of, 65–71;
    evasion, 70; resistance to, 62,
    65, 68, 146–150; substitutes
    and exemptions, 63–64. *See
    also* Bounties; Commutation;
    New York City draft riots.
Constitutional Union party, 6, 45
Contrabands, 126–127, 134

Contracting, war, 93–94, 166; and
    distribution of wealth, 103
Cooke, Jay, 96–97
Cooper Shop Refreshment Saloon,
    113
Copperheads, 49, 52–54, 144,
    161–162, 164
Cox, Annie, 83
Crittenden Compromise, 9–10
Crittenden, John, 8–9
Culture and society, antebellum,
    26–31; in wartime, 83–90

Daly, Maria Lydig, 133, 178
Davis, Jefferson, 8, 32, 33, 54–55,
    146, 151–152, 178, 183
Days of Shoddy, 17–18
Death and mourning, 75–77. *See
    also* Casualties.
Deerfield, Mass., 65
DeForest, John William, 88
Delaware, 165, 175–176
Democratic party, 18, 20, 45, 49,
    52–54, 128, 143–144, 196. *See
    also* specific elections; Copper-
    heads; individual names.
Desertion, 167–168
Detroit, 149
Dicey, Edward, 77–78
Dickinson, Anna, 154, 189
Dickinson, Emily, 87
Dix, Dorothea, 106, 117
Douglas, Stephen A., 6, 7, 20, 45
Douglass, Frederick, 131, 133, 174
Draft. *See* Conscription.
Dred Scott decision, 7
Drum Taps (Whitman), 87
Dwight, John Sullivan, 84, 85

Economic growth and
    development: antebellum,
    24–26; distribution of wealth,
    103–104; impact of Civil War
    on, 100–103, 184–186; postwar,
    181, 183. *See also* Economic
    policies.

Economic policies, 19, 20, 45, 46–47; finance, 94–99, 185–186; impact on American economy, 99–101; and supply system, 93–94. *See also* Banking; Taxation; Confederacy; Salmon P. Chase.

Education, antebellum, 30–31

8th Massachusetts, 25

Einhorn, Robin, 188

Elections: of 1856, 5; of 1860, 5–8; of 1862, 49–50, 53, 129, 143; of 1863, 161–162; of 1864, 160, 162–166

Ellsworth, Elmer, 75

Emancipation, 20, 125–129, 175–176; and women, 153–154

Emancipation Proclamation, 34, 42, 49, 50, 53, 86, 125, 128–131

Emerson, Ralph Waldo, 77, 86

Enlistment and recruiting, 15–16, 23, 47–48, 56–62, 166–168; calls for men, 12, 40, 46, 58, 60, 61, 65, 166–167; Confederacy, 32; Quakers, 89–90. *See also* Black soldiers.

Enrollment Act, 51, 62, 65

Ex parte Merryman, 142–143

Exemptions, conscription, 63, 69, 71

Fahnestock, George W., 133

Farragut, David G., 40

Fifteenth Amendment, 190, 192

54th Massachusetts, 132

Fillmore, Millard, 5

Finance. *See* Economic policies.

Fincher's Trades' Review, 67–68

Forrest, Edwin, 84

Forrest, Nathan Bedford, 173

Fort Donelson, 40

Fort Henry, 40

Fort Pickens, 11

Fort Pillow, 173

Fort Sumter, 11–12, 14, 179

Fort Wagner, 132

Forten, Charlotte, 125, 136

Fourteenth Amendment, 184, 192

Fredericksburg, battle of, 42

Fredrickson, George, 86

Freedmen and Soldiers' Relief Association, 137

Freedmen's Bureau, 176, 183, 192

Fremont, John C., 5, 126, 162

Frisch, Michael, 85

Fry, James B., 62–63, 69

Gardner, Alexander, 77

Gettysburg Address, 55, 77, 195

Gettysburg, battle of, 43, 55, 121

Ginzberg, Lori, 190

Glatthaar, Joseph, 197

Graham, Sylvester, 30

Grand Army of the Republic, 197

Grant, Ulysses S., 40, 43, 51, 118, 159–160, 178–179

Gratz, Rebecca, 76

Greeley, Horace, 127, 163

Greenbacks, 47, 96–97, 181

Guerrilla warfare, 149, 152

Habeas corpus, writ of, 14, 20, 45, 46, 142–143, 145, 181–182

Habeas Corpus Act, 51

Halleck, Henry, 41, 159

Hamlin, Hannibal, 162

Hammond, William, 116

Hampton Roads, 41

Harper's Magazine, 93

Hawks, Esther Hill, 118, 135

Hawthorne, Nathaniel, 87

Hicks, Thomas H., 13, 14

Hill, Ambrose Powell, 41

Hoge, Jane C., 124, 153, 172

Holmes, Oliver Wendell, Jr., 196

Homestead Act, 52, 99, 102, 185

Hooker, Joseph, 42–43

Hospital Sketches (Alcott), 86

Howard, Oliver O., 176

Howells, William Dean, 87

Hubbell, Katherine, 83

Hughes, John, 89

Hunter, David, 126

Illinois, 50, 52, 142
Immigrants, 23; antebellum, 28–29; and military participation, 58, 67; and violence, 147–150
Indiana, 50, 52, 142
Intellectuals, reactions to the war, 85–88
Iowa, 192

Jackson, Thomas J. ("Stonewall"), 41, 43
Jacksonville, Ill., 90
Jacobs, Harriet, 137–138
James, Henry, Jr., 87
Johnson, Andrew, 162, 192
Johnston, Joseph E., 160
Joint Committee on the Conduct of the War, 48
Jones, William Thomas, 80

Kansas-Nebraska Act, 7
Keckley, Elizabeth, 137
Keller, Morton, 183
Kentucky, 13, 14, 165, 175, 187
Knights of the Golden Circle, 144

Labor. See Workers.
Lee, Robert E., 41–43, 51, 159–160, 178–179
Legal Tender Act, 47, 96, 97, 99
Lincoln, Abraham, 95, 111, 178, 195; assassination of, 179; attitudes toward blacks and slavery, 7, 19, 134, 174, 191; background, 7, 19; and black troops, 130; and civil liberties, 14, 48, 142–143; compared with Jefferson Davis, 151–152; and 1860 election, 5–8; and emancipation, 49, 50, 125–129; and Fort Sumter crisis, 11–12; and Gettysburg Address, 55, 77; inauguration of, 10–11;

and military, 40–43, 159–161; and politics, 44–45, 51, 162–165; and propaganda, 120; and Reconstruction, 168–170; and recruiting, 166–167; responses to secession, 9; and seamstresses, 106. See also Emancipation Proclamation.
Linderman, Gerald, 76–77
Literature, 86–88
Livermore, Mary, 124, 153, 172, 178, 190
Localism, 27, 31, 72, 79, 111–114, 123, 171–172, 180, 182–183, 188
Louisiana, 128, 175
Louisville, 10
Loyal Publication Society, 119
Lynch, John, 80

Manassas Junction, 21. See also Bull Run.
Manhood and masculinity, 57, 77, 190–191
Manufacturing, 24, 25; impact of the Civil War, 101–102
Maryland, 9, 13–14, 175–176, 187
Massachusetts, 30, 174, 187
McClellan, George B., 40–42, 46, 53–54, 163–165
McDowell, Irvin, 21
McPherson, James M., 195
Meade, George, 43, 159–160
Medicine, 115–117. See also Nursing.
Meigs, Montgomery C., 92, 102
Melville, Herman, 87
Merrimack, 41
Merryman, John, 142–143
Mexican War, 32
Michigan, 70, 192
Militia Act, 47–48, 60, 62, 130
Milliken's Bend, 132
Minnesota, 192
Miss Ravenel's Conversion from Secession to Loyalty (DeForest), 88

Missouri, 9, 13, 14, 175
Missouri Compromise, 9
Mitchell, Reid, 79, 191
Mitchell, Silas Wier, 116
Monitor, 41
Monkkonen, Eric, 90
Morford, Henry, 17–18, 88
Morrill Land Grant College Act,
    88, 99, 185–186
Morse, Samuel, 119

National Banking Act, 51, 97,
    99, 185
National Freedmen's Relief
    Association, 135
National Union party, 162
Nationalism, 16, 31, 123, 188, 195
Navy, 24–25, 40, 42; and black
    sailors, 130
Neely, Mark E., Jr., 145
New Jersey, 165, 175
New Orleans, 40
New York Bible Society, 112
New York City, 116, 170–171,
    172, 187; almshouse, 107;
    antebellum education, 30; and
    black troops, 173; blacks in,
    137; conscription in, 61;
    Copperheads, 53; desegregation
    in, 174; draft evasion in, 70;
    1862 elections, 50; and secession
    crisis, 14; violence in, 148, 154
New York City draft riots, 65,
    147–148, 155, 156
New York Daily Tribune, 79, 127
*New York Musical World and
    Review,* 84
New York World, 143
Newspapers, 31, 78–79, 84, 143,
    146. *See also* specific
    newspapers.
Nightingale, Florence, 117
North Carolina, 12
Nursing, 106, 117–118, 188

Ohio, 50, 52, 142

Olmsted, Frederick Law, 122
Otis, Esther, 135

Pacific Road Bill, 185
Pamphleteering, 118–120, 123,
    143, 164
Party structure, North vs. South,
    44
Pendleton, George, 164
Peninsula Campaign, 40–41
Pennsylvania, 50, 70, 148, 187
Pensions, 183
Perryville, battle of, 42
Petersburg, 160, 178
Philadelphia, 53, 118, 187; arrests
    in, 90; blacks in, 131–132, 134,
    136–137, 139; civic ritual, 121;
    desegregation in, 174–175;
    Great Central Fair, 171; House
    of Correction, 107; seamstresses,
    106; and secession crisis, 14;
    Union League, 119; violence
    in, 149–150; voluntarism,
    112–113, 114; workingmen's
    assembly, 10
Philadelphia Evening Journal, 143
Photography, 79
Pickett's Charge, 43
Politics, participation, 28. *See also*
    specific elections, parties.
Pope, John, 41
Population: North vs. South,
    22–23
Port Hudson, 132
Port Washington, Wisc., 149
Pringle, Cyrus, 64
Prisoner-of-war camps, 168
Proclamation of Amnesty and
    Reconstruction, 169–170

Quakers, 64, 89–90, 113

Railroads, 24, 101–102
Reconstruction, 162, 168–170, 192,
    193

Recruiting. *See* Enlistment and
recruiting.
Religion, 195–196; antebellum,
27, 29; and voluntarism, 112;
and war effort, 89
Republican ideology, 194–195
Republican party, 5, 20, 44, 45,
162, 196; economic policies, 18,
99, 186; and emancipation, 126
Rhode Island, 192
Richmond, 178
Rituals, civic, 27, 78, 90–91,
120–121, 180
Rock, John, 174
Rosecrans, William S., 42
Russell, William Howard, 21
Rutland, Vt., 148

Sanitary Fairs, 124, 170–172
Savannah, 160
Secession crisis, 8–14
Secret societies, 142, 144–145, 156,
164–165
Separation by the war, 77–83
Seward, William H., 19, 48, 51,
179
Seymour, Horatio, 53
Shaw, Robert Gould, 132–133
Sherman, John, 127–128
Sherman, William T., 127–128,
159–161, 164, 178
Shiloh, battle of, 40
6th Massachusetts Volunteers, 13
Slavery. *See* Blacks; Emancipation;
Emancipation Proclamation;
Abraham Lincoln.
Smalls, Robert, 130
Smith, Hannah, 80
Smith, J. L., 76
Society for the Diffusion of
Political Knowledge, 119–120
Soldiers' Aid Societies, 112
Sons of Liberty, 144–145
South. *See* Confederacy.
South Carolina, 8, 11, 135
Sports, 84–85

Springfield Armory, 93, 187
Springfield, Ill., 121, 179
Springfield, Mass., 85, 187
Springfield Republican, 129
Stanton, Edwin M., 60, 62, 93, 130
Stanton, Elizabeth Cady, 153
Star of the West, 11
Stevens, Thaddeus, 45, 47
Stille, Charles Janeway, 37, 43
Storey, Wilbur, 104
Stowe, Harriet Beecher, 75
Strong, George Templeton, 86,
172, 195
Studebaker, Clement, 103
Substitutes, 63, 71
Sumner, Charles, 138, 192
Supreme Court, 7, 142–143, 174.
See also specific cases.

Taney, Roger, 142–143
Taxation, 20, 28, 47, 95–97, 166,
181, 185–186
Taylor, Suzi King, 135–136
Teachout, Webster, 80
Tennessee, 12, 128, 159, 175
Theater, 84
Thirteenth Amendment, 175
Thompson, Jennie, 80, 83
Thumb, Tom, 84
Tilden, Samuel, 119
Tocqueville, Alexis de, 109
Total war, 157–158, 161, 182
Tourgee, Albion, 196
Trautwine, Susan, 76
Trent, 96
Trumbull, Lyman, 48
Truth, Sojourner, 136, 174
Tubman, Harriet, 135
Twain, Mark, 87
Tweed, Boss, 187

Uncle Tom's Cabin, 75
United States Christian
Commission, 111, 122
United States Sanitary
Commission, 94, 110–112, 116,

117, 122–123, 170–172;
Northwestern Branch, 114,
124, 153, 170

Vallandigham, Clement L., 49,
53, 143–144, 146, 161, 164
Values and beliefs, 194–196
Vicksburg, Miss., 40, 43, 51, 55
Violence and disorder, 29, 139,
146–150; in the Confederacy,
152
Virginia, 9, 12, 128
Voluntarism, 16–17, 109–115,
122–124, 170–172; antebellum,
109–110; and blacks, 135–136;
and women, 110–112, 123–124
Volunteer Refreshment Saloon,
113

Wade-Davis Bill, 169–170
Washington, D. C., 18, 138, 174,
178–179
West Virginia, 175
Wharton, Katherine Brinley, 80
Wheelock, Julia, 80
Whetten, Harriet Douglas,
117–118
Whitman, Walt, 86, 87, 117

Wisconsin, 70, 192
Wister, Sarah Butler, 83
Woman's National Loyal League,
153–154, 189–190
Women: and disorder, 154–155;
economic experiences, 82–83,
105–107; impact of Civil War
on, 188–190; and nursing,
117–118; political role, 16, 27,
152–155; Southern, 154; and
voluntarism, 17, 110–112,
114–115, 123–124, 135, 172;
and wartime separations, 81–83
Women's Central Association of
Relief, 110, 118, 124, 153, 190
Women's Christian Temperance
Union, 190
Wood, Fernando, 14, 53
Woodward, George, 161
Workers: antebellum, 29; and
disorder, 148, 156; and draft
resistance, 148; and
emancipation, 128; impact of
Civil War on, 193–194; labor
unions, 104; and secession
crisis, 9; and wartime economy,
103–105. See also Women.
Workingmen's Protective Union,
106

A NOTE ON THE AUTHOR

J. Matthew Gallman was born in Baltimore and grew up in Chapel Hill, North Carolina. He studied at Princeton University and at Brandeis University, where he received a Ph.D. in American history. In addition to numerous articles on the Civil War home front and on colonial American demography, he is the author of *Mastering Wartime: A Social History of Philadelphia During the Civil War.* He is now associate professor of history at Loyola College, Maryland.